A Century of Lyrics
1550–1650

A Century of Lyrics
1550–1650

Edited by
D. C. Whimster

Granger Index Reprint Series

Originally published by
EDWARD ARNOLD & CO.
London

BOOKS FOR LIBRARIES PRESS
FREEPORT, NEW YORK

First published 1938 by Edward Arnold & Co.

Reprinted 1971 by arrangement

To

E. E. W.

INTERNATIONAL STANDARD BOOK NUMBER:
0-8369-6276-1

LIBRARY OF CONGRESS CATALOG CARD NUMBER:
79-160911

PRINTED IN THE UNITED STATES OF AMERICA

Preface

In this selection of lyrics from 1550 to 1650, the interest or delight of the poem has been the chief criterion. The lyrics are arranged in a roughly chronological order, because I feel that when seen in their proper sequence they illustrate the changing ideas of the time. For this reason some poets, such as Donne and Herbert, who are usually omitted from anthologies of so-called " Elizabethan " lyrics, have been included.

Brief notes on points of explanation and appreciation have been printed with the poems ; they should enable the anthology to be used for private reading and learning, as well as providing a starting-point for discussion and composition. Where the context of the poem, and particularly of a song from a play, has seemed interesting, part of the scene or a short account of the situation has been given.

I have verified the text of all the lyrics (except Nos. 5, 19, 42, 43) from the earliest manuscripts and editions ; and all the poems are unabridged and, except for spelling and punctuation, unaltered.

D. C. Whimster.

Harrow, 1938.

Contents

			Page
1.	The Lover Complaineth . . .	Sir Thomas Wyatt . .	19
2.	A Praise of his Love	Earl of Surrey . . .	21
3.	Description of Virtue	Nicholas Grimald . .	22
4.	"Cupid and my Campaspe played"	John Lyly	23
5.	The Lady Greensleeves . . .	Anonymous	24
6.	A Litany	Sir Philip Sidney . .	27
7.	"My prime of life is but a frost of cares"	Chidiock Tichborne .	29
8.	"What pleasure have great princes"	Anonymous	30
9.	"My golden locks time hath to silver turned"	George Peele . . .	31
10.	The Ploughman's Song . . .	Nicholas Breton . .	33
11.	"Spring, the sweet spring" . .	Thomas Nashe . . .	34
12.	The Passionate Shepherd to his Love	Christopher Marlowe .	35
13.	The Nymph's Reply to the Shepherd	Sir Walter Raleigh .	36
14.	Winter	William Shakespeare .	37
15.	New Prince, New Pomp . . .	Robert Southwell . .	38
16.	The Triple Fool	John Donne . . .	39
17.	"Autumn hath all the summer's fruitful treasure"	Thomas Nashe . . .	40
18.	"Sigh no more, ladies" . . .	William Shakespeare .	41
19.	"Happy were he"	Earl of Essex . . .	42
20.	To the Month of September . .	Sir John Davies . .	42
21.	"Come away, come away, death"	William Shakespeare .	43
22.	"Slow, slow, fresh fount" . .	Ben Jonson	44
23.	"Queen and huntress" . . .	Ben Jonson	45
24.	To Colin Clout	Anthony Munday . .	46
25.	"Gorbo, as thou camest this way"	Michael Drayton . .	47
26.	"Thule, the period of cosmography"	Thomas Weelkes . .	49
27.	"When thou must home to shades of underground"	Thomas Campion . .	50
28.	"When to her lute Corinna sings"	Thomas Campion . .	50
29.	"The man of life upright" . .	Thomas Campion . .	51

[6]

30. The Angler's Song . . . . *William Basse* . . . 52
31. " Golden slumbers kiss your eyes " *Thomas Dekker* . . 54
32. The Basket-maker's Song . . *Thomas Dekker* . . 55
33. " Weep you no more sad foun-
    tains " . . . . *Anonymous* 56
34. The Passionate Man's Pilgrimage *Sir Walter Raleigh* . . 57
35. " Sister awake, close not your
    eyes " . . . . *Anonymous* 59
36. " Fain would I change that note " *Tobias Hume* . . . 60
37. " Fools, they are the only nation " *Ben Jonson* 61
38. " There is a garden in her face " *Thomas Campion* . . 62
39. " Shepherds all, and maidens fair " *John Fletcher* . . . 63
40. " All ye woods, and trees and
    bowers " . . . . *John Fletcher* . . . 64
41. " Fear no more the heat o' the
    sun " . . . . *William Shakespeare* . 65
42. A Religious Use of Taking
    Tobacco . . . . *Anonymous* 66
43. " The sea hath many thousand
    sands " . . . . *Anonymous* 67
44. " Lay a garland on my hearse " *Beaumont and Fletcher* . 68
45. " Let not the sluggish sleep " . *Anonymous* 68
46. A Bellman's Song . . . . . *Thomas Campion* . . 68
47. " Full fathom five thy father lies " *William Shakespeare* . 69
48. " Call for the robin-redbreast and
    the wren " . . . . . . *John Webster* . . . 70
49. Epitaph on Salathiel Pavy . . *Ben Jonson* 70
50. " What is our life ? " . . . . *Sir Walter Raleigh* . 71
51. " Roses, their sharp spines being
    gone " . . . . *Shakespeare and Fletcher* 72
52. " Jack and Joan " . . . . . *Thomas Campion* . . 73
53. " Now winter nights enlarge " . *Thomas Campion* . . 74
54. " To his sweet lute Apollo sung " *Thomas Campion* . . 75
55. " Arm, arm, arm, arm ! " . . *John Fletcher* . . . 76
56. " Sweet Suffolk owl " . . . *Thomas Vautor* . . 78
57. " To see a strange outlandish fowl " *Henry Farley* . . . 78
58. " The faery beam upon you " . *Ben Jonson* 79
59. A Christmas Carol . . . . . *George Wither* . . . 80
60. " Sweet was the song the Virgin
    sung " . . . . *Anonymous* 84
61. Epitaph on the Countess Dowager
    of Pembroke . . . . . . *William Browne* . . 84
62. " This world a hunting is " . . *William Drummond* . 85
63. " Hark, now everything is still " *John Webster* . . . 85
64. A Hymn to God the Father . . *John Donne* . . . 86

65. " Haymakers, rakers, reapers, and
mowers " . . . . *Thomas Dekker* . . 87
66. " Hence all you vain delights " . *John Fletcher* . . . 88
67. The Fairies' Farewell . . . . *Bishop Corbet* . . . 89
68. " All this night shrill chanticler " *William Austin* . . 92
69. " Fly hence, shadows " . . . *John Ford* 93
70. " A rose, as fair as ever saw the
north " . . . . *William Browne* . . 93
71. In Praise of Ale . . . . . *Thomas Bonham* . . 94
72. Hos ego versiculos . . . . *Francis Quarles* . . 95
73. The Quip . . . . *George Herbert* . . 96
74. Virtue . . . . *George Herbert* . . 98
75. The Pulley . . . . *George Herbert* . . 99
76. Love . . . . *George Herbert* . . 100
77. " Oh sorrow, sorrow, say where
thou dost dwell ? " . . . . *Samuel Rowley* . . 100
78. " O thou that sleep'st like pig in
straw " . . . . *Sir William Davenant* . 101
79. " My limbs I will fling " . . . *William Strode* . . . 102
80. " Why so pale and wan, fond
lover ? " . . . . *Sir John Suckling* . . 103
81. " We show no monstrous croco-
dile " . . . . *Jasper Mayne* . . . 104
82. " The glories of our blood and
state " . . . . *James Shirley* . . . 105
83. Epigram : On Sir Francis Drake *Anonymous* . . . 106
84. " If all the world were paper " . *Anonymous* . . . 106
85. Song of the Beggars . . . . *Richard Brome* . . . 107
86. " Go, lovely rose " . . . . *Edmund Waller* . . 108
87. " Yet if his majesty " . . . . *Anonymous* . . . 109
88. " Say, bold but blessed thief " . *Anonymous* . . . 110
89. A Thanksgiving to God, for his
House . . . . *Robert Herrick* . . 112
90. To Meadows . . . . . . *Robert Herrick* . . 114
91. The Night-piece, to Julia . . . *Robert Herrick* . . 115
92. His Poetry His Pillar . . . . *Robert Herrick* . . 116
93. To Daffodils . . . . . . *Robert Herrick* . . 117
94. To Lucasta, Going to the Wars . *Richard Lovelace* . . 118
95. Peace . . . . *Henry Vaughan* . . 118
96. The Retreat . . . . . . *Henry Vaughan* . . 119
97. De Morte . . . . *Anonymous* . . . 121
98. The Coronet . . . . . . *Andrew Marvell* . . 122
99. A Contemplation upon Flowers . *Bishop King* . . . 123
100. " The lark now leaves his watery
nest " . . . . *Sir William Davenant* . 123

Introduction

I

A poem always tells us something about the mind and feelings of its writer. The songs in this book, however, tell us much more. Their authors were not, most of them, professional poets, nor were they unsociable men, cut off from the active life of their time. They were courtiers, soldiers, actors, or adventurers, playing their part in an age that was full of excitement and change. So the songs that they write reflect what ordinary people felt and thought. It will help us to understand their poems if we look first at the world in which they lived.

It was a world that in only a few generations had gone through the most amazing changes ; and men in Elizabeth's reign must have felt as if they had come out from a dark and tangled wood into the sunlight and the fields. Less than a hundred years before, men's thoughts and actions had been hemmed in by authority that they never dared to question. Now the barriers had miraculously fallen, opening up a world of freedom and freshness and opportunity.

First of all, the power of the barons was gone, ruined by their own quarrels in the tedious and wasteful Wars of the Roses. Men now owed allegiance only to the sovereign, who saw to it that no individual noble was allowed to become over-powerful. This brought a feeling of security to the land. England was united as a nation, with a strong ruler at its head.

Again, the authority of the Church had greatly decreased. Men of the Middle Ages had been like children, accepting the traditional faiths with unquestioning obedience. Now they were growing up, and as they learnt to test what the Church taught, they found much that was unworthy or untrue. The re-discovery of Greek literature was one of the chief causes of this new desire for freedom. The Greeks had been scientific inquirers after knowledge ; a man like Socrates never accepted anything upon authority, but questioned and searched until he reached the truth. It is difficult for us to imagine the thrilling experience that this idea brought to mediæval men. " The students rush to Greek letters, they endure watching, fasting, toil and hunger in pursuit of them," and there were crowded and enthusiastic audiences to listen to the first Professor of Greek at Oxford.

The effect that this longing for accurate knowledge had on religion was soon felt. Whereas for hundreds of years most men had only known of the Gospels at second-hand, from hearing them chanted in church, scholars now set to work to re-translate them accurately and clearly. In 1516 Erasmus' translation, although only into Latin, sold over a hundred thousand copies in France alone. By 1540, English Bibles were in every parish church. Many people were for the first time interpreting Christ's message for themselves.

The quick spread of this new learning would have been impossible without printing. In 1424 the University of Cambridge had only 122 books in its library, all of them laboriously written out by hand. By Elizabeth's time even the poorest scholar could hope to own some printed books, and new opinions had a chance of spreading fast.

Men's outlook was also greatly widened by tales of new lands beyond the seas. Until 1492 England was on the edge of the civilized world, and frequently cut off from it by war with France. But with the discovery of America all hopes looked westward. Europe seemed tired and dull,

> " a little world
> Of petty men grown mean and wise,"

compared with the glorious vision of Eldorado and the dream-cities of the west. What did it matter that the Spaniards had a long start of us, and that they claimed America almost as a Spanish possession ? England was well placed for a challenge

[10]

to their supremacy, and discovered with joy that the treasure ships were easily plundered. Piracy became a gentleman's occupation, and every village in England was thrilled by stories of heroic battles and daring raids, of strange customs and creatures, and of the gold that awaited any man with a stout ship and a ready sword.

The real triumph of Henry VIII and Elizabeth is that they succeeded in centring all these feelings on themselves. Henry had been greeted with universal joy when he came to the throne. " Could you but see ", says a letter written in the first days of his reign, " how nobly he is bearing himself, how wise he is, his love for all that is good and right, and specially his love for all men of learning, you would need no wings to fly into the light of this new-risen star." The vision faded, for as his power increased he grew brutal and unrestrained, but his popularity never disappeared.

After the confusion of Edward VI's reign, and the bitterness and strife of Mary's, Elizabeth's accession in 1558 seemed to introduce once more the Golden Age that had been hoped for from Henry VIII. Elizabeth was young and attractive, skilled in music, able to read Greek and to talk Latin, French, and Italian ; fond of splendid dresses and of pageants and plays, never too weary to hunt or to dance with her courtiers. With all this she could understand a political situation as well as her advisers, and was untiring in her love for England and her efforts to make the country peaceful and rich. As she told her last Parliament, " though you have had, and may have, many mightier and wiser princes sitting in this seat, yet you never had, nor shall have one that will love you better ".

No queen was better known to her people, for every summer she went on interminable progresses through the countryside, receiving addresses and petitions, and being entertained with pageants and plays of all kinds. She had always a welcome for anything that was witty or spectacular or well carried out, whether it was a comedy or a firework display, a grave and learned speech or a clever retort, a daring raid on the Spanish fleet or a delicate piece of diplomacy. Every man could hope for a chance to show his worth to Elizabeth and her nobles, many of whom had risen to greatness in just the same way, with nothing but their own merits to commend them. " The spacious days of great Elizabeth " were great largely because of this : new men, new ideas, new discoveries were eagerly welcomed and readily accepted.

Before the end of her reign, however, some of the glory had departed, and men began again to feel that life was flat and uninteresting ; they were ready for a change. As an outspoken writer put it,

> " Where are all thy beauties now, all hearts enchaining ?
> Whither are thy flatterers gone with all their feigning ?
> All fled ; and thou alone still here remaining."

The queen was losing the reverence of her subjects ; and the tragic rebellion of the young Earl of Essex occurred because he thought of Elizabeth as an old woman who would not take advice. After her death all were willing to welcome James I as, in the glorious spring weather of 1603, he rode slowly south from Scotland. But the outlook was not very favourable. England had loved the queen for her vivacious and enthralling personality, and in any case she would not have been an easy person to succeed. Unluckily, James was a complete contrast to her. He was cautious and uninspiring, too conceited about his learning, and full of theories about the high rights of kings. Also, the England that he came to rule was entirely changed from that of fifty years before. The middle classes, the merchants and townsmen, had taken the place of the old aristocratic families, with Parliament as their mouthpiece. With that change had grown up a greater seriousness in religion, a strict belief in the importance of personal conduct and the wickedness of elaborate ritual, that we call Puritanism.

The Puritans believed that they had a right to their own opinions in politics and in religion, whereas James claimed that kings have a divine right to govern exactly as they think fit, without advice or interference. So it is not surprising that his reign is full of quarrels between king and Parliament, between the king's supporters and the Puritans.

When Charles I came to the throne in 1625, Parliament tried to make sure from the start that he would grant liberty to his subjects. Perhaps he was obstinate in his refusal, but they were certainly unreasonable in their demands. With right and wrong on both sides, the Civil War, when it came in 1642, was bound to be bitter and long drawn out. Although in the end the Puritans won, the execution of Charles I lost them many supporters, and made it certain that eventually his son would succeed to the throne.

II

The publication of Tottel's *Miscellany*, in 1557, marks the true beginning of the period in lyrical poetry. It consists largely of love lyrics by courtiers like Wyatt and Surrey, who wrote not for publication but for their own pleasure. Their poems were probably handed round among their friends for a few weeks and then forgotten, unless some enterprising printer was lucky enough to get hold of them. Many of these courtiers' poems were anonymous, or published after the death of their author ; it became an essential of every gentleman to be able to write a sonnet or a love lyric, but not quite respectable for him to have them sold for gain to the general public.

These early poems were probably not meant to be sung, but songs set to music soon came into fashion, for there has been no age in English history when singing has been more popular. Beggars had their special songs ; there were musical street-cries for every kind of trade, songs for worktime and play-time, songs for taverns and for church festivals, songs belonging to particular districts, and ballads that were hawked round the whole country and eagerly bought and sung.

> " Since singing is so good a thing,
> I wish all men would learn to sing,"

says one of the greatest musicians of the time, William Byrd ;

and his wish has never been nearer coming true than in the reign of Elizabeth.

Not only did men sing, but they knew a good deal about music. In the barbers' shops a lute was hung up for customers to strum upon while they waited their turn. In the villages one might hear " the beautiful music of violas and pandoras, for in all England it is the custom that even in small villages the musicians wait on you for a small fee. In the morning about wakening time they stand outside the chamber playing religious hymns." Pedlars and minstrels, like Autolycus in Shakespeare's *Winter's Tale*, went about singing and selling ballads, and wherever they went they found country people who could sing a part-song at sight. In a citizen's house, too, the table would be cleared after a meal and the songbooks produced. Here, from a schoolbook of 1573, is a typical conversation :

FATHER. Roland, shall we have a song ?

ROLAND. Yea, sir. Where be your books of music ? For they be the best corrected.

FATHER. They be in my chest ; you shall find them in a little till at the left hand. Behold, there be fair songs of four parts.

ROLAND. Who shall sing with me ?

FATHER. You shall have company enough : David shall make the bass, John the tenor, and James the treble. Begin. James, take your tune. Go to ; for what do you tarry ?

From an Introduction to Music comes the sad story of a man who actually could not take part in singing. " But supper being ended, and music-books (according to the custom) being brought to the tables, the mistress of the house presented me with a part, earnestly requesting me to sing. But when, after many excuses, I protested unfeignedly that I could not, everyone began to wonder. Yea, some whispered to others, demanding how I was brought up." Is it surprising that he went off early the next morning to a music-master, to make up the gap in his education ?

It was fortunate that at a time when there was this universal feeling for music, and when England under Queen Elizabeth was at the height of her national pride, there were men who could rise to the occasion, and were capable of writing magnificent songs. After Tottel's *Miscellany* there had been an interval of about twenty years, when very little was produced. But with the appearance of Spenser's *Shepherd's Calendar*, in 1579, there began one of the greatest periods of English literature, to which every type of writer contributed. No longer were the courtiers the only or the best lyric-writers, though men like Sir Walter Raleigh and Sir John Davies carried on the tradition. Musicians sometimes wrote the words as well as the music of their songbooks, and some of them, particularly Campion, were fine poets. Play-writers like Marlowe and Nashe and Dekker, though their lives were wretched and riotous, could nevertheless write love-songs and lullabies of the most delicate freshness and gentleness. Lyly, Shakespeare and Fletcher knew that a song well sung upon the stage would never fail to please their audience, and some of the finest lyrics were written to accompany the acting of a wedding or a funeral, a dance or a procession. Even men living in fear of their lives, like the Roman Catholics Southwell and Chidiock Tichborne, were willing and able to record their feeling in moving poetry.

Although the authors were so varied in type, there are three things that almost all the lyrics written in Elizabeth's and James's reigns have in common. First of all, they have a quality of tunefulness that was altogether lost by the end of the seventeenth century. Even poems by unknown or undistinguished authors have lines that seem to sing themselves, like

> " Sweet Suffolk owl, so trimly dight
> With feathers, like a lady bright,"

or,

> " All in our gowns of green so gay
> Into the park a-maying,"

or,

> " Though poor and plain our diet,
> Yet merry it is and quiet."

There are very few poems in the songbooks that lack this tunefulness, perhaps because with the popularity of music all men had a sense of metre and rhythm.

Again, the great majority of the poems have a feeling of

freshness, and give the idea that the world is a simple and cheerful place, full of sunshine and happiness.

> " It were a most delightful thing
> To live in a perpetual spring,"

and many of the Elizabethans seem in their songs to achieve it. Only a few of the lyric-writers, such as Raleigh and Donne, appear to think of life as complicated or depressing. The others are thrilled with the zest and joy of the moment,

> " And, fortune's fate not fearing,
> Sing sweet in summer morning."

The third common characteristic is the personal note that runs through most of the poems. The subject may be the conventional and unenterprising one of hopeless love, or a longing for the contented life of the fields ; but there are always some phrases that show first-hand observation, and make us feel that the author is keenly interested, and not just writing on a decorative but unimportant subject. The poems talk of shepherds and nymphs, of Coridon and Phillida, who sound distant and unreal ; but the shepherd offers his nymph " fair linèd slippers for the cold ", and Phillida " with garlands gay was made the Lady of the May ". It is clear that the writers are really thinking of everyday life in English farms and villages, where " old wives a-sunning sit ", and Jack and Joan

> " Skip and trip it on the green,
> And help to choose the Summer Queen,"

and in winter " Marian's nose looks red and raw ". Even in poems where such descriptions as these would be out of place, a line like " And what she said, I know it, I ", gives the same vivid and personal feeling.

These three qualities, of tunefulness, of freshness, and of personal interest, are most noticeable between 1580 and 1620, when most of the lyrics in plays and songbooks were written. A change, however, was taking place. To some extent the poems of one man, John Donne, were responsible, but far more important was the changing spirit of the times. Puritanism was making men more serious and reflective, and the Court had lost much of its gaiety and graceful love of verses. England as a whole was giving up its widespread interest in singing, so that before 1630 the publishing of songbooks had ceased. The Puritans disapproved of theatres ; plays grew fewer and worse, long before the actual closing of the theatres in 1642. Authors became more professional and self-conscious, altering and correcting their work and publishing it in collected editions. All these changes left little place for the smooth, sunlit songs that had filled songbooks and plays. They had to make way for " the strong lines ", as Isaac Walton called them, " that are now in fashion in this critical age ".

The country was gradually taking sides with King or Parliament, and poems too were separating into two distinct types. Either they were quiet and deeply religious, the work of country-dwellers like Herbert and Vaughan, men who thought continually and with much agony of mind about their own relations with God ; or they were boisterous and confident, the gay songs of cavaliers like Suckling, Lovelace and Davenant. As the Civil War grew more bitter, there was little time or inclination for song-writing, and by 1660 the tradition had almost entirely died out. For the next hundred years poetry was full of mature good sense, of finely polished phrases and urbane language ; but the youthful freshness and tunefulness of the Elizabethans had altogether vanished.

A Century of Lyrics

1550-1650

1

The Lover complaineth the unkindness of his love

My lute, awake ! perform the last
Labour that thou and I shall waste,
  And end that I have now begun ;
For when this song is sung and past,
  My lute, be still, for I have done.

As to be heard where ear is none,
As lead to grave in marble stone,
  My song may pierce her heart as soon.
Should we then sigh, or sing, or moan ?
  No, no, my lute, for I have done.

The rocks do not so cruelly
Repulse the waves continually,
  As she my suit and affection ;
So that I am past remedy,
  Whereby my lute and I have done.

Proud of the spoil that thou hast got
Of simple hearts thorough love's shot,
  By whom, unkind, thou hast them won,
Think not he hath his bow forgot,
  Although my lute and I have done.

[19]

Vengeance shall fall on thy disdain,
That makest but game on earnest pain.
  Think not alone under the sun
Unquit to cause thy lovers plain,
  Although my lute and I have done.

Maychance thee lie withered and old,
In winter nights that are so cold,
  Plaining in vain unto the moon ;
Thy wishes then dare not be told.
  Care then who list, for I have done.

And then may chance thee to repent
The time that thou hast lost and spent
  To cause thy lovers sigh and swoon ;
Then shalt thou know beauty but lent,
  And wish and want as I have done.

Now cease, my lute ! this is the last
Labour that thou and I shall waste,
  And ended is that we begun ;
Now is this song both sung and past.
  My lute, be still, for I have done.

Tottel's *Miscellany*.   SIR THOMAS WYATT.

As lead to grave in marble stone, like trying to cut marble with a soft
    metal such as lead.
Who list, whoever will.

  This poem was printed in 1557, in Tottel's *Miscellany*, the first
collection of poems published in English. Many of them were by
Sir Thomas Wyatt, who had been very popular at the court of Henry

VIII, and had died in 1542. He and the Earl of Surrey changed the whole course of English poetry by introducing Italian ideas about metre, rhyme, and subject. But though the subject of this poem is a conventional one in Italian poetry, lines like " In winter nights that are so cold " show a vigorous and simple imagination that is not at all conventional.

2

A Praise of his Love : wherein he reproveth them that compare their ladies with his

Give place, ye lovers here before,
    That spent your boasts and brags in vain ;
My lady's beauty passeth more
    The best of yours, I dare well sayn,
Than doth the sun the candle-light,
Or brightest day the darkest night.

And thereto hath a troth as just
    As had Penelope the fair.
For what she saith, ye may it trust,
    As it by writing sealèd were ;
And virtues hath she many mo,
Than I with pen have skill to show.

I could rehearse, if that I would,
    The whole effect of Nature's plaint,
When she had lost the perfect mould,
    The like to whom she could not paint ;
With wringing hands how she did cry,
And what she said, I know it, I.

[21]

I know she swore with raging mind,
   Her kingdom only set apart,
There was no loss, by law of kind,
   That could have gone so near her heart ;
And this was chiefly all her pain :
She could not make the like again.

Sith Nature thus gave her the praise,
   To be the chiefest work she wrought,
In faith, methink, some better ways
   On your behalf might well be sought,
Than to compare (as ye have done)
To match the candle with the sun.

Tottel's *Miscellany*.   HENRY HOWARD, EARL OF SURREY.

Sayn, the old infinitive of " say ".
Troth, faith, trustworthiness.
Penelope, the wife of Ulysses, and faithful to him throughout his ten
   long years of wandering, after the fall of Troy.
Mo, more.
Sith, since.

   Surrey was a great friend of Wyatt, though much younger. He
too was popular in Henry VIII's court, but in 1547 was accused of
treason and beheaded. This magnificently arrogant poem is, like
Wyatt's, conventional in subject, but has personal touches and almost
slangy phrases, such as " And what she said, I know it, I ".

3. Description of Virtue

What one art thou, thus in torn weeds yclad ?
" Virtue, in price whom ancient sages had."
Why poorly 'rayed ? " For fading goods past care."
Why double-faced ? " I mark each fortune's fare."
This bridle, what ? " Mind's rages to restrain."
Tools why bear you ? " I love to take great pain."

Why wings ? " I teach above the stars to fly."
Why tread you death ? " I only cannot die."

Tottel's *Miscellany*.   NICHOLAS GRIMALD.

Had in price, considered precious.
'Rayed, arrayed, dressed.
I mark each fortune's fare, I see how each man's fortune changes.

4

Cupid and my Campaspe played
At cards for kisses ; Cupid paid.
He stakes his quiver, bow, and arrows,
His mother's doves, and team of sparrows ;
Loses them too ; then down he throws
The coral of his lip, the rose
Growing on's cheek (but none knows how) ;
With these, the crystal of his brow,
And then the dimple of his chin ;
All these did my Campaspe win.
At last, he set her both his eyes ;
She won, and Cupid blind did rise.
  O Love ! has she done this to thee ?
  What shall (alas !) become of me ?

Campaspe, 1584.   JOHN LYLY.

A song in a play " By the only rare poet of that time, the witty,
comical, facetiously quick and unparalleled John Lyly ". He intro-
duced into the court a new style of talking and writing, full of clever
comparisons and far-fetched allusions. It was called Euphuism, and
became most popular, " she who spoke not Euphuism being as little
regarded at Court as if she could not speak French ". Here is a taste
of it, from a letter from Lyly to Queen Elizabeth : " I know not what
crab took me for an oyster, that in the midst of the sunshine of your
most gracious aspect hath thrust a stone between the shells, to eat me
alive that only live on dead hopes."

5

A New Courtly Sonnet of the Lady Greensleeves ; to the new tune of Greensleeves

Greensleeves was all my joy,
Greensleeves was my delight ;
Greensleeves was my heart of gold,
And who but Lady Greensleeves.

Alas, my Love ! ye do me wrong
  To cast me off discourteously ;
And I have lovèd you so long,
  Delighting in your company.

I have been ready at your hand,
  To grant whatever you would crave ;
I have both wagèd life and land,
  Your love and goodwill for to have.

I bought thee kerchers to thy head,
  That were wrought fine and gallantly ;
I kept thee both at board and bed,
  Which cost my purse well favouredly.

I bought thee petticoats of the best,
  The cloth so fine as fine might be ;
I gave thee jewels for thy chest,
  And all this cost I spent on thee.

Thy smock of silk, both fair and white,
  With gold embroidered gorgeously ;
Thy petticoat of sendal right ;
  And thus I bought thee gladly.

Thy girdle of gold so red,
  With pearls bedeckèd sumptuously ;
The like no other lasses had,
  And yet thou wouldst not love me.

Thy purse and eke thy gay gilt knives,
  Thy pincase gallant to the eye ;
No better wore the burgess wives,
  And yet thou wouldst not love me.

Thy crimson stockings all of silk,
  With gold all wrought above the knee ;
Thy pumps as white as was the milk,
  And yet thou wouldst not love me.

Thy gown was of the grassy green,
  Thy sleeves of satin hanging by,
Which made thee be our harvest queen ;
  And yet thou wouldst not love me.

Thy garters fringèd with the gold,
  And silver aglets hanging by,
Which made thee blithe for to behold ;
  And yet thou wouldst not love me.

My gayest gelding I thee gave,
  To ride wherever likèd thee ;
No lady ever was so brave,
  And yet thou wouldst not love me.

My men were clothèd all in green,
  And they did ever wait on thee ;
All this was gallant to be seen,
  And yet thou wouldst not love me.

[25]

They set thee up, they took thee down,
   They served thee with humility ;
Thy foot might not once touch the ground,
   And yet thou wouldst not love me.

For every morning when thou rose,
   I sent thee dainties orderly,
To cheer thy stomach from all woes ;
   And yet thou wouldst not love me.

Thou couldst desire no earthly thing
   But still thou hadst it readily ;
Thy music still to play and sing,
   And yet thou wouldst not love me.

And who did pay for all this gear
   That thou didst spend when pleasèd thee ?
Even I that am rejected here,
   And thou disdain'st to love me.

Well, I will pray to God on high,
   That thou my constancy mayst see,
And that, yet once before I die,
   Thou wilt vouchsafe to love me.

Greensleeves, now farewell, adieu !
   God I pray to prosper thee !
For I am still thy lover true,
   Come once again and love me.

Greensleeves was all my joy,
   Greensleeves was my delight ;

> *Greensleeves was my heart of gold,*
> *And who but Lady Greensleeves.*

A Handful of Pleasant Delights, 1584.   ANONYMOUS.

Kerchers, scarves.
Sendal, silk.
Pincase, a quite expensive present, since pins were only newly intro-
    duced, and very popular.
Burgess wives, wives of rich merchants.
Pumps, shoes.
Aglets, tags.

   A Handful of Pleasant Delights is a ballad book, of which only one
copy is known. It contains poems " newly devised to the newest
tunes that are now in use " ; but the tunes are only referred to, not
printed in full. The verse " Greensleeves is all my joy " is used as a
chorus after each verse of the song.

6. A Litany

Ring out your bells, let mourning shows be spread,
For Love is dead.
   All Love is dead, infected
With plague of deep disdain ;
   Worth, as nought worth, rejected,
And Faith fair scorn doth gain.
   From so ungrateful fancy,
   From such a female frenzy,
      From them that use men thus,
      Good Lord deliver us !

Weep, neighbours, weep, do you not hear it said
That Love is dead ?
   His death-bed, peacock's folly,
His winding-sheet is shame,

[27]

His will, false-seeming holy,
His sole executor, blame.
  From so ungrateful fancy,
  From such a female frenzy,
    From them that use men thus,
    Good Lord deliver us !

Let dirge be sung and trentals rightly read,
For Love is dead.
  Sir Wrong his tomb ordaineth
My mistress' marble heart,
  Which epitaph containeth,
" Her eyes were once his dart."
  From so ungrateful fancy,
  From such a female frenzy,
    From them that use men thus,
    Good Lord deliver us !

Alas, I lie ; rage hath this error bred,
Love is not dead.
  Love is not dead, but sleepeth
In her unmatchèd mind,
  Where she his counsel keepeth,
Till due desert she find.
  Therefore from so vile fancy,
  To call such wit a frenzy,
    Who Love can temper thus,
    Good Lord deliver us !

Certain Sonnets.   Sir Philip Sidney.

Trentals, services every day for thirty days, for the souls of the dead.
My mistress' marble heart. The first edition has " My mistress Marble-
    heart ", making Marble-heart into a kind of nickname ; but it
    is the heart that must be the tomb and contain the epitaph.
Temper, restrain.

Sidney is one of the most romantic figures of Elizabeth's reign.   He was a handsome courtier, an able soldier, a fine poet and prose-writer, the greatest of the " Courtly Makers " ; one that loved poetry so much that whenever he heard the old ballads, " I found my heart moved more than with a trumpet ".   He was killed in battle in 1586, after refusing water so that a dying soldier might get relief from pain. His noble life and death made the Elizabethans remember him as the highest example of courtly chivalry.

> " Sidney the hope of land strange,
> Sidney the flower of England,
> Sidney the spirit heroic,
> Sidney is dead !   O dead ! dead ! "

7

My prime of life is but a frost of cares,
  My feast of joy is but a dish of pain,
My crop of corn is but a field of tares,
  And all my good is but vain hope of gain.
My life is fled, and yet I saw no sun ;
And now I live, and now my life is done.

The Spring is past, and yet it hath not sprung,
  The fruit is dead, and yet the leaves be green,
My youth is gone, and yet I am but young,
  I saw the world, and yet I was not seen.
My thread is cut, and yet it is not spun ;
And now I live, and now my life is done.

East's *Madrigals*.   CHIDIOCK TICHBORNE.

Chidiock Tichborne was a Roman Catholic who joined in the Babington Plot, a conspiracy to assassinate Elizabeth and set Mary Queen of Scots on the throne of England.   This poem is said to have been written just before his execution in 1586.

8

What pleasure have great princes,
  More dainty to their choice,
Than herdmen wild, who careless
  In quiet life rejoice ?
And fortune's fate not fearing,
Sing sweet in summer morning.

Their dealings plain and rightful
  Are void of all deceit ;
They never know how spiteful
  It is to kneel and wait
On favourite presumptuous,
Whose pride is vain and sumptuous.

All day their flocks each tendeth,
  At night they take their rest,
More quiet than who sendeth
  His ship into the east,
Where gold and pearl are plenty,
But getting, very dainty.

For lawyers and their pleading
  They 'steem it not a straw ;
They think that honest meaning
  Is of itself a law ;
Where conscience judgeth plainly,
They spend no money vainly.

O happy who thus liveth,
  Not caring much for gold,
With clothing which sufficeth

To keep him from the cold.
Though poor and plain his diet,
Yet merry it is and quiet.

Byrd's *Psalms, Sonnets, and Songs*, 1588.   ANONYMOUS.

Getting, very dainty, making money is very difficult.
'Steem, esteem.

9

The original occasions of the yearly Triumphs in England

These annual exercises in arms, solemnised the 17th day of November, were first begun by the right virtuous and honourable Sir Henry Lea, Master of Her Highness' Armoury, who voluntarily vowed (unless infirmity, age, or other accident did impeach him) to present himself at the tilt armed, the day aforesaid, yearly, there to perform in honour of her sacred Majesty the promise he formerly made. The lords and gentlemen of the court, incited by so worthy an example, have ever since yearly assembled in arms accordingly ; though true it is that the author of that custom (being now by age overtaken) in the thirty-third year of her Majesty's reign resigned, and recommended that office unto the right noble George Earl of Cumberland.

On the 17th day of November, Anno 1590, this honourable gentleman, together with the Earl of Cumberland, having first performed their service in arms, presented themselves unto her Highness, at the foot of the stairs under her gallery window in the tilt yard at Westminster, where at that time her Majesty did sit.

Her Majesty, beholding these armed knights coming towards her, did suddenly hear a music so sweet and secret as everyone thereat greatly marvelled. The music was accompanied by these verses.

My golden locks time hath to silver turned ;
  (O time too swift, and swiftness never ceasing)
My youth 'gainst time and age hath ever spurned,
  But spurned in vain ; youth waneth by increasing.
Beauty, strength, youth are flowers but fading seen ;
Duty, faith, love are roots and ever green.

My helmet now shall make a hive for bees,
  And lovers' songs shall turn to holy psalms.
A man-at-arms must now serve on his knees,
  And feed on prayers, that are old age's alms
But though from court to cottage I depart,
My saint is sure of mine unspotted heart.

And when I sadly sit in homely cell,
  I'll teach my swains this carol for a song,
" Blest be the hearts that wish my sovereign well,
  Curst be the souls that think her any wrong."
Goddess, allow this agèd man his right,
To be your beadsman now, that was your knight.

Certain presents being with great reverence delivered into
her Majesty's own hands, Sir Henry Lea himself, disarmed,
offered up his armour at the foot of her Majesty's crowned
pillar, and kneeling upon his knees presented the Earl of
Cumberland, humbly beseeching she would be pleased to
accept him for her knight, to continue the yearly exercises.
Her Majesty graciously accepting of that offer, this aged
knight armed the Earl, and mounted him upon his horse.
That being done, he put upon his own person a side-coat
of black velvet pointed under the arm, and covered his head
(in lieu of a helmet) with a button cap of the country fashion.

Beadsman, one who offers up prayers for his benefactor.

The poem is by George Peele, and was set to music by Dowland ;
the account is shortened from *Honors Military and Civil* (1602).

10. The Ploughman's Song

In the merry month of May,
In a morn by break of day,
Forth I walked by the wood side,
Whereas May was in his pride.
There I spièd all alone
Phillida and Coridon.
Much ado there was, God wot,
He would love and she would not.
She said, never man was true :
He said, none was false to you.
He said, he had loved her long ;
She said, love should have no wrong.
Coridon would kiss her then ;
She said, maids must kiss no men
Till they did for good and all.
Then she made the shepherd call
All the heavens to witness truth,
Never loved a truer youth.
Thus with many a pretty oath,
Yea and nay, and faith and troth,
Such as silly shepherds use,
When they will not love abuse,
Love, which had been long deluded,
Was with kisses sweet concluded ;
And Phillida with garlands gay
Was made the Lady of the May.

The Honourable Entertainment   NICHOLAS BRETON.
at Elvetham, 1591.

Silly, simple.

Phillida and Coridon are conventional names given to shepherds
in Greek and Latin poetry ; it became the fashion to give the characters
in love poetry these names.

In 1591 Elizabeth visited the Earl of Hertford at Elvetham.   Though she came only for three days, he had had the house enlarged and a lake dug, with islands on which entertainments were prepared. On the second morning three musicians in country attire sang songs beneath the Queen's window, and one, dressed as a ploughman, sang this song of Phillida and Coridon. That evening there was a great banquet, and a firework display on the lake. The next morning the Queen departed with all ceremony—

> " O come again, sweet beauty's sun ;
> When thou art gone, our joys are done."

11

Spring, the sweet spring, is the year's pleasant king ;
Then blooms each thing, then maids dance in a ring,
Cold doth not sting, the pretty birds do sing :
    Cuckoo, jug-jug, pu-we, to-witta-woo.

The palm and may make country houses gay.
Lambs frisk and play, the shepherds pipe all day,
And we hear aye birds tune this merry lay :
    Cuckoo, jug-jug, pu-we, to-witta-woo.

The fields breathe sweet, the daisies kiss our feet,
Young lovers meet, old wives a-sunning sit ;
In every street these tunes our ears do greet ;
    Cuckoo, jug-jug, pu-we, to-witta-woo.
      Spring, the sweet spring !

Summer's Last Will and Testament.   THOMAS NASHE.

Enter Ver (Spring) with his train, overlaid with suits of green moss, representing short grass, singing, is the stage direction ; and this is his cheerful song.

The cuckoo and the nightingale both make spring resound with their songs, and the pewit or lapwing is heard then more frequently than later in the year ; but what about the owl ?

The Passionate Shepherd to his Love

Come live with me and be my love,
And we will all the pleasures prove,
That valleys, groves, hills and fields,
Woods, or steepy mountain yields.

And we will sit upon the rocks,
Seeing the shepherds feed their flocks,
By shallow rivers to whose falls
Melodious birds sing madrigals.

And I will make thee beds of roses
And a thousand fragrant posies,
A cap of flowers, and a kirtle
Embroidered all with leaves of myrtle ;

A gown made of the finest wool
Which from our pretty lambs we pull ;
Fair linèd slippers for the cold,
With buckles of the purest gold ;

A belt of straw and ivy buds,
With coral clasps and amber studs ;
And if these pleasures may thee move,
Come live with me and be my love.

The shepherds' swains shall dance and sing
For thy delight each May morning.
If these delights thy mind may move,
Then live with me and be my love.

CHRISTOPHER MARLOWE.

The Nymph's Reply to the Shepherd

If all the world and love were young,
And truth in every shepherd's tongue,
These pretty pleasures might me move
To live with thee, and be thy love.

Time drives the flocks from field to fold,
When rivers rage, and rocks grow cold,
And Philomel becometh dumb ;
The rest complain of cares to come.

The flowers do fade, and wanton fields
To wayward winter reckoning yields ;
A honey tongue, a heart of gall,
Is fancy's spring, but sorrow's fall.

Thy gowns, thy shoes, thy beds of roses,
Thy cap, thy kirtle, and thy posies
Soon break, soon wither, soon forgotten,
In folly ripe, in reason rotten.

Thy belt of straw and ivy buds,
Thy coral clasps and amber studs,
All these in me no means can move
To come to thee, and be thy love.

But could youth last and love still breed,
Had joys no date nor age no need,
Then these delights my mind might move
To live with thee, and be thy love.

SIR WALTER RALEIGH.

Try reading the last two poems together, alternate verses of each ; do Raleigh's verses exactly fit Marlowe's ? And is the nymph's reply a convincing answer ?

14. Winter

When icicles hang by the wall,
  And Dick the shepherd blows his nail,
And Tom bears logs into the hall,
  And milk comes frozen home in pail ;
When blood is nipped, and ways be foul,
Then nightly sings the staring owl,
Tu-whit, tu-who ! a merry note,
While greasy Joan doth keel the pot.

When all aloud the wind doth blow,
  And coughing drowns the parson's saw,
And birds sit brooding in the snow,
  And Marian's nose looks red and raw,
When roasted crabs hiss in the bowl,
Then nightly sings the staring owl,
Tu-whit, tu-who ! a merry note,
While greasy Joan doth keel the pot.

Love's Labour's Lost, 1594–5.   WILLIAM SHAKESPEARE.

Keel, cool by ladling.
Saw, wise saying.
Crab, crab-apple.

A perfectly detailed picture of life in a country village, in very few words. Nowhere does Shakespeare directly say that it was cold weather ; but notice how many colourful facts he gives that point to the same thing. Look back to Nash's poem on Spring (No. 11) ; does he make any vivid pictures ? To write a companion poem on Summer or Autumn, what facts would you give ?

[37]

15. New Prince, New Pomp

Behold, a silly tender Babe
   In freezing winter night
In homely manger trembling lies ;
   Alas, a piteous sight !

The inns are full ; no man will yield
   This little pilgrim bed,
But forced he is with silly beasts
   In crib to shroud his head.

Despise him not for lying there,
   First, what he is enquire ;
An orient pearl is often found
   In depth of dirty mire.

Weigh not his crib, his wooden dish,
   Nor beasts that by him feed ;
Weigh not his mother's poor attire,
   Nor Joseph's simple weed.

This stable is a Prince's court,
   The crib his chair of state ;
The beasts are parcel of his pomp,
   The wooden dish his plate.

The persons in that poor attire
   His royal liveries wear ;
The Prince himself is come from heaven ;
   This pomp is prizèd there.

With joy approach, O Christian wight,
   Do homage to thy King ;

And highly praise his humble pomp,
Which he from heaven doth bring.

Saint Peter's Complaint.   ROBERT SOUTHWELL.

Orient, from the east, of fine quality.
Weigh, consider.
Weed, clothes.
Parcel, part.
Wight, man.

Robert Southwell was a Roman Catholic priest of the order of Jesuits, which was suspected and hated by Elizabeth's government. A law was passed declaring that any Englishman who became a Catholic priest was a traitor. Though Southwell knew this, he risked his life for his faith by coming to England, and was arrested and hanged in 1595.

16. The Triple Fool

I am two fools, I know,
For loving, and for saying so
   In whining poetry ;
But where's that wise man, that would not be I,
   If she would not deny ?
Then as th'earth's inward narrow crooked lanes
Do purge sea water's fretful salt away,
   I thought, if I could draw my pains,
Through rhyme's vexation, I should them allay ;
Grief brought to numbers cannot be so fierce,
For he tames it, that fetters it in verse.

But when I have done so,
Some man, his art and voice to show,
   Doth set and sing my pain,
And, by delighting many, frees again
   Grief, which verse did restrain.

[39]

To love and grief, tribute of verse belongs,
But not of such as pleases when 'tis read,
  Both are increasèd by such songs :
For both their triumphs so are publishèd,
And I, which was two fools, do so grow three ;
Who are a little wise, the best fools be.

Songs and Sonnets.   JOHN DONNE.

This poem is a complete contrast to all the poems so far. It is much
more complicated, more full of meaning, harsher in its metre and
phrasing, more personal. Donne's influence, although it only spread
gradually, was immense. After men had read a line like " Busy old
fool, unruly sun ", or " For God's sake hold your tongue, and let me
love ", it was difficult for them, whether they liked Donne's style or
not, to go on writing smooth even verse in quite the same way as
before.

17

Autumn hath all the summer's fruitful treasure ;
Gone is our sport, fled is poor Croydon's pleasure.
Short days, sharp days, long nights come on apace,
Ah who shall hide us from the winter's face ?
Cold doth increase, the sickness will not cease,
And here we lie, God knows, with little ease.
  From winter, plague, and pestilence, good Lord,
    deliver us !

London doth mourn, Lambeth is quite forlorn ;
Trades cry, Woe worth, that ever they were born.
The want of term is town and city's harm ;
Close chambers we do want, to keep us warm.
Long banishèd must we live from our friends ;
This low-built house will bring us to our ends.
  From winter, plague, and pestilence, good Lord,
    deliver us !

Summer's Last Will and Testament.   THOMAS NASHE.

Woe worth, alas !

Near the end of Nashe's play, Will Summer, the hero, says,
" Farewell, my friends, Summer bids you farewell.
Weep heavens, mourn earth, here Summer ends."
Here the satyrs and wood-nymphs carry him out, singing as he came in.
This is Summer's farewell song.

" The want of term " may show that this song was put into the
play in 1598, when there was an outbreak of plague, and the law-
courts held their autumn term at St. Albans instead of London. It
is hard for us to realise now either the horror that the plague meant
in a crowded city like London, or the difficulties and boredom that
winter brought, with the lack of fresh meat or vegetables, and problems
of heating and of transport.

18

Sigh no more, ladies, sigh no more,
　Men were deceivers ever ;
One foot in sea, and one on shore,
　To one thing constant never.
　　Then sigh not so,
　　But let them go,
　And be you blithe and bonny,
Converting all your sounds of woe
　Into Hey nonny, nonny.

Sing no more ditties, sing no mo
　Of dumps so dull and heavy ;
The fraud of men was ever so,
　Since summer first was leavy.
　　Then sigh not so,
　　But let them go,
　And be you blithe and bonny,
Converting all your sounds of woe
　Into Hey nonny, nonny.

Much Ado about Nothing, 1598–9.　WILLIAM SHAKESPEARE.

Happy were he could finish forth his fate
  In some unhaunted desert, most obscure
From all societies, from love and hate
  Of worldly folk ; then might he sleep secure ;
Then wake again, and give God ever praise,
  Content with hips and haws and bramble-berry ;
In contemplation spending all his days,
  And change of holy thoughts to make him merry ;
Where, when he dies, his tomb may be a bush,
Where harmless robin dwells with gentle thrush.

EARL OF ESSEX.

This simple poem is found in a manuscript now in Manchester, and is supposed to have been sent to Queen Elizabeth in a letter from the Earl of Essex, when he was in Ireland in 1599. He had been a great favourite with the Queen, but grew arrogant and vain. He was sent to Ireland to suppress a rebellion, but came back with nothing done. In a last desperate effort Essex planned a revolt against the Queen, but his supporters melted away, and he was condemned for treason and executed.

Did he mean what he says in this poem ? Possibly he did, for the moment ; but his longing for power, and his proud restlessness, would have made life away from the court impossible for him.

20. To the Month of September

Each month hath praise in some degree ;
Let May to others seem to be
In sense the sweetest season ;
September thou art best to me,
And best doth please my reason.

But neither for thy corn and wine
Extol I those mild days of thine,
Though corn and wine might praise thee ;
Heaven gives thee honour more divine,
And higher fortunes raise thee.

Renowned art thou (sweet month) for this,
Emong thy days her birthday is ;
Grace, plenty, peace and honour
In one fair hour with her were born ;
Now since, they still her crown adorn,
And still attend upon her.

Hymns of Astraea, in Acrostic   SIR JOHN DAVIES.
  Verse, 1599.

In 1599, when Queen Elizabeth was sixty-six years old, Sir John
Davies published his twenty-six *Hymns to Astraea*, praising the Queen,
and each making with its initial letters the words Elisabetha Regina.
It is a proof of the personal love and admiration that the Queen still
received ; and all the more so since the poems are fresh and natural.
In this poem the spelling of " emong " was a possible alternative.

21

Enter CLOWN.

DUKE. O, fellow ! come, the song we had last night.
Mark it, Cesario ; it is old and plain ;
The spinsters and the knitters in the sun,
And the free maids that weave their threads with bones,
Do use to chant it ; it is silly sooth,
And dallies with the innocence of love,
Like the old age.
  CLOWN. Are you ready, sir ?
  DUKE. Ay ; prithee, sing.

[43]

Come away, come away, death,
  And in sad cypress let me be laid.
Fly away, fly away, breath;
  I am slain by a fair cruel maid.
My shroud of white, stuck all with yew,
      O prepare it.
My part of death, no one so true
      Did share it.

Not a flower, not a flower sweet
  On my black coffin let there be strown;
Not a friend, not a friend greet
  My poor corpse, where my bones shall be thrown.
A thousand thousand sighs to save,
      Lay me, O where
Sad true lover never find my grave,
      To weep there.

DUKE. There's for thy pains.
CLOWN. No pains, sir; I take pleasure in singing, sir.
DUKE. I'll pay thy pleasure, then.
CLOWN. Truly, sir, and pleasure will be paid, one time
or another.
  DUKE. Give me now leave to leave thee.

Twelfth Night, 1599–1600.   WILLIAM SHAKESPEARE.

Cypress, probably a dark wooden coffin.

  Does this song really fit the Duke's description of it? Some critics
have suspected that it does not belong here, and that the original song
has been lost.

22

Slow, slow, fresh fount; keep time with my salt tears;
  Yet slower yet, O faintly, gentle springs:

List to the heavy part the music bears ;
   Woe weeps out her division, when she sings.
      Droop, herbs and flowers ;
      Fall, grief, in showers.
      Our beauties are not ours.
            O, I could still,
   Like melting snow upon some craggy hill,
         Drop, drop, O drop,
   Since nature's pride is now a withered daffodil.

Cynthia's Revels, 1600.   BEN JONSON.

Division, a rapid passage of music, which Woe lengthens out, because
   of her sadness.

Echo, a nymph of the woods, who could only repeat the words of
others, fell in love with Narcissus.   But he was too vain, and pleased
only to watch his own reflection in a forest pool.   For love of this
he pined and died, and was changed to the flower that bears his name.
Echo, in the play *Cynthia's Revels*, is given a voice and words to weep
for her " withered daffodil ", beside the pool that caused his doom.

23

   Queen and huntress, chaste, and fair,
   Now the sun is laid to sleep,
   Seated in thy silver chair,
   State in wonted manner keep ;
         Hesperus entreats thy light,
         Goddess, excellently bright.

   Earth, let not thy envious shade
   Dare itself to interpose ;
   Cynthia's shining orb was made
   Heaven to clear, when day did close ;
         Bless us then with wishèd sight,
         Goddess, excellently bright.

Lay thy bow of pearl apart,
And thy crystal-shining quiver ;
Give unto the flying hart
Space to breathe, how short soever ;
  Thou that mak'st a day of night,
  Goddess, excellently bright.

Cynthia's Revels, 1600.   BEN JONSON.

Hesperus, the Evening Star.
Cynthia, the goddess of the moon, was also the goddess of hunting.

24. To Colin Clout

Beauty sat bathing by a spring,
  Where fairest shades did hide her ;
The winds blew calm, the birds did sing,
  The cool streams ran beside her.
My wanton thoughts enticed mine eye
  To see what was forbidden ;
But better memory said fie,
  So vain desire was chidden.

Into a slumber then I fell,
  When fond imagination
Seemèd to see, but could not tell
  Her feature or her fashion.
But even as babes in dreams do smile,
  And sometime fall a-weeping,
So I awaked, as wise this while,
  As when I fell a-sleeping.

Pilkington's *First Book of*   ANTHONY MUNDAY.
  Songs or Airs.

BATTE. Gorbo, as thou camest this way
    By yonder little hill,
  Or as thou through the fields didst stray,
    Saw'st thou my Daffodil ?

  She's in a frock of Lincoln green,
    The colour maids delight,
  And never hath her beauty seen,
    But through a veil of white.

  Than roses richer to behold
    That trim up lovers' bowers,
  The pansy and the marigold,
    Though Phœbus' paramours.

GORBO. Thou well describest the daffodil ;
    It is not full an hour,
  Since by the spring near yonder hill
    I saw that lovely flower.

BATTE. Yet my fair flower thou didst not meet,
    Nor news of her didst bring,
  And yet my Daffodil's more sweet
    Than that by yonder spring.

GORBO. I saw a shepherd that doth keep
    In yonder field of lilies,
  Was making (as he fed his sheep)
    A wreath of daffodillies.

[47]

BATTE.   Yet Gorbo thou delud'st me still,
          My flower thou didst not see ;
       For know my pretty Daffodil
          Is worn of none but me.

          To show itself but near her seat,
             No lily 'is so bold,
          Except to shade her from the heat,
             Or keep her from the cold.

GORBO.   Through yonder vale as I did pass,
             Descending from the hill,
          I met a smirking bonny lass,
             They call her Daffodil ;

          Whose presence, as she went along,
             The pretty flowers did greet,
          As though their heads they downward bent,
             With homage to her feet.

          And all the shepherds that were nigh,
             From top of every hill,
          Unto the valleys low did cry,
             " There goes sweet Daffodil."

BATTE.   Ay gentle shepherd, now with joy
             Thou all my flocks dost fill,
          That's she alone, kind shepherd boy ;
             Let us to Daffodil.

Poems Lyric and Pastoral.   MICHAEL DRAYTON.

Phœbus' paramours, the flowers that the sun loves.

The shepherds, in Drayton's poem, are just finishing their yearly

[48]

feast, and now the shepherdesses join them. Batte ("a wittier wag in all the world's not found") has been asked to sing a song. He cannot see his lovely Daffodil at the feast, and asks Gorbo, who is to sing the undersong, whether he has seen her.

26

Thule, the period of cosmography,
  Doth vaunt of Hecla, whose sulphurious fire
Doth melt the frozen clime and thaw the sky ;
  Trinacrian Aetna's flames ascend not higher.
These things seem wondrous, yet more wondrous I,
Whose heart with fear doth freeze, with love doth fry.

The Andalusian merchant, that returns
  Laden with cochineal and China dishes,
Reports in Spain how strangely Fogo burns
  Amidst an ocean full of flying fishes.
These things seem wondrous, yet more wondrous I,
Whose heart with fear doth freeze, with love doth fry.

Madrigals, 1600.   THOMAS WEELKES.

Although the main subject of this song is the conventional one of the pains of love, the chief interest to us lies in the comparison with geographical marvels. Thule here evidently means Iceland, the furthest place on the Elizabethan map, which, he says, boasts of the volcano Hecla, which is as active as Etna in Sicily (Trinacria). The Spanish merchant, coming back from a trading expedition in the East, tells of " the island called by the Portugals Ilha da Fogo, that is the burning island, in the north side whereof is a consuming fire ", as the account of Drake's famous voyage round the world describes it. In the same story we are told of the flying-fishes " whereof some fell into our boat ; wherehence they could not rise again for want of moisture, for when their wings are dry they cannot fly ".

[49]   D

When thou must home to shades of underground,
   And there arrived, a new admirèd guest,
The beauteous spirits do engirt thee round,
   White Iopè, blithe Helen and the rest,
To hear the stories of thy finished love
From that smooth tongue, whose music hell can move ;

Then wilt thou speak of banqueting delights,
   Of masques and revels which sweet youth did make,
Of tourneys and great challenges of knights,
   And all these triumphs for thy beauty's sake.
When thou hast told these honours done to thee,
Then tell, O tell, how thou didst murder me.

Rosseter's *Book of Airs*, 1601.   THOMAS CAMPION.

Iopè, or Cassiopeia, boasted that her daughter Andromeda was more
   lovely than the Nereids, the nymphs of the sea. Their revenge
   was to send her down to the shadowy realm of Hades ; but later
   she was set among the stars.
Helen, for whose beauty the Greeks besieged and sacked Troy.

This song has a magnificent climax. The smooth narrative of the
first verse works up in the second to the clear-sounding " banqueting ",
" tourneys ", " challenges ", as it describes the gay revels in the lady's
honour. So far all is complimentary to her ; but then after a pause
comes the crash of " murder ", with all the shock of unexpectedness.

When to her lute Corinna sings,
Her voice revives the leaden strings,
And doth in highest notes appear,
As any challenged echo clear.
But when she doth of mourning speak,
E'en with her sighs the strings do break.

And as her lute doth live or die,
Led by her passion, so must I.
For when of pleasure she doth sing,
My thoughts enjoy a sudden spring ;
But if she doth of sorrow speak,
E'en from my heart the strings do break.

Rosseter's *Book of Airs*, 1601.   THOMAS CAMPION.

Thomas Campion was one of the few Elizabethan song-writers
that wrote both words and music. " In these English airs ", he says
in his introduction, " I have chiefly aimed to couple my words and
notes lovingly together ".

Even without the music one can see from this song his tunefulness,
and his skill in making the second verse exactly parallel to the first,
so that the same tune will fit the sense and the words of both verses.
Notice for instance the suddenly clear and cheerful sound of the fourth
lines (" challenged echo clear ", " sudden spring "), and the way in
which the rather far-fetched idea in each verse is brought to a climax.

Philip Rosseter, who wrote half the songs in their *Book of Airs*, was
Campion's greatest friend. Campion, in his will, " left all that he
had unto Mr. Philip Rosseter, and wished it had been far more ".
It was £22.

29

The man of life upright,
   Whose guiltless heart is free
From all dishonest deeds
   Or thought of vanity :

The man whose silent days
   In harmless joys are spent,
Whom hopes cannot delude,
   Nor sorrow discontent :

That man needs neither towers
  Nor armour for defence,
Nor secret vaults to fly
  From thunder's violence.

He only can behold
  With unaffrighted eyes
The horrors of the deep
  And terrors of the skies.

Thus scorning all the cares
  That fate or fortune brings,
He makes the heaven his book,
  His wisdom heavenly things.

Good thoughts his only friends,
  His wealth a well-spent age,
The earth his sober inn
  And quiet pilgrimage.

Rosseter's *Book of Airs*, 1601.   THOMAS CAMPION.

This was a very popular song, although the words are not the same
in all the collections. For instance, one version begins—
      " The man of life upright,
          Whose cheerful mind is free
        From weight of impious deeds
          And yoke of vanity ".

30. The Angler's Song

As inward love breeds outward talk,
The hound some praise, and some the hawk ;
Some better pleased with private sport
Use tennis ; some a mistress court ;

But these delights I neither wish,
Nor envy, while I freely fish.

Who hunts, doth oft in danger ride ;
Who hawks, lures oft both far and wide ;
Who uses games, may often prove
A loser ; but who falls in love,
  Is fettered in fond Cupid's snare ;
  My angle breeds me no such care.

Of recreation there is none
So free as fishing is alone ;
All other pastimes do no less
Than mind and body both possess ;
  My hand alone my work can do,
  So I can fish and study too.

I care not, I, to fish in seas,
Fresh rivers best my mind do please,
Whose sweet calm course I contemplate,
And seek in life to imitate ;
  In civil bounds I fain would keep,
  And for my past offences weep.

And when the timorous trout I wait
To take, and he devours my bait,
How poor a thing sometimes I find
Will captivate a greedy mind ;
  And when none bite, I praise the wise,
  Whom vain allurements ne'er surprise.

But yet though while I fish I fast,
I make good fortune my repast,
And thereunto my friend invite,
In whom I more than that delight ;

Who is more welcome to my dish,
Than to my angle was my fish.

As well content no prize to take
As use of taken prize to make ;
For so our Lord was pleasèd when
He fishers made fishers of men ;
   Where (which is in no other game)
   A man may fish and praise his name.

The first men that our Saviour dear
Did choose to wait upon him here
Blest fishers were ; and fish the last
Food was, that he on earth did taste :
   I therefore strive to follow those
   Whom he to follow him hath chose.

Walton's *Compleat Angler*.   WILLIAM BASSE.

How many arguments are there here for fishing ? And can you
think of any more, or any arguments against it ? The poem makes
it sound an ideal occupation ; as Coridon says when the song is over,
" Well sung, brother ; you have paid your debt in good coin ; we
anglers are all beholden to the good man that made this song."

31

Golden slumbers kiss your eyes,
Smiles awake you when you rise.
Sleep, pretty wantons, do not cry,
And I will sing a lullaby :
Rock them, rock them, lullaby.

Care is heavy, therefore sleep you ;
You are care, and care must keep you.

Sleep, pretty wantons, do not cry,
And I will sing a lullaby :
Rock them, rock them, lullaby.

Patient Grissil, 1603.   THOMAS DEKKER.

Grissil, or Grisilde, is the great example of the patient wife. In
Dekker's play, her husband, a rich marquis, tests her faithfulness by
sending her away and threatening to take her children from her. She
goes to her father the basket-maker, who welcomes her and the babes.

"Lay them both softly down. Grissil, sit down.
Laneo, fetch you my lute. Rock thou the cradle.
Cover the poor fool's arm. I'll charm their eyes
To take a sleep by sweet-tuned lullabies ".

Then he sings, and the words of the song are full of meaning. The
babies are his care, and must be carefully guarded. When they awoke
they found, not smiles, but the scowls of their supposed murderers,
come to take them away. But they were spared, and Grissil's faith-
fulness survived all the tests.

32. The Basket-maker's Song

Art thou poor, yet hast thou golden slumbers ?
    O sweet content !
Art thou rich, yet is thy mind perplexèd ?
    O punishment !
Dost thou laugh to see how fools are vexèd
To add to golden numbers, golden numbers ?
O sweet content ! O sweet, O sweet content !
    Work apace, apace, apace, apace ;
    Honest labour bears a lovely face ;
Then hey nonny nonny, hey nonny nonny !

Canst drink the waters of the crispèd spring ?
    O sweet content !

Swim'st thou in wealth, yet sink'st in thine own tears?
   O punishment!
Then he that patiently want's burden bears
No burden bears, but is a king, a king!
O sweet content! O sweet, O sweet content!
   Work apace, apace, apace, apace;
   Honest labour bears a lovely face;
Then hey nonny nonny, hey nonny nonny!

Patient Grissil, 1603.   THOMAS DEKKER.

33

Weep you no more sad fountains,
   What need you flow so fast?
Look how the snowy mountains
   Heaven's sun doth gently waste.
      But my sun's heavenly eyes
      View not your weeping,
      That now lies sleeping
      Softly, now softly lies
         Sleeping.

Sleep is a reconciling,
   A rest that peace begets;
Doth not the sun rise smiling,
   When fair at even he sets?
      Rest you then, rest, sad eyes,
      Melt not in weeping,
      While she lies sleeping
      Softly, now softly lies
         Sleeping.

Dowland's *Last Book of Songs*   ANONYMOUS.
   or *Airs*, 1603.

This song is not at all clear in meaning. Roughly, it must be—

[56]

"Just as the sun makes the snow melt, so my lady, because she will not accept me, makes me weep. But now she is sleeping, and sleep brings peace and harmony. So I shall weep no more, but be tranquil."

But the exact meaning does not matter so much, compared with the gentleness and tranquillity of the words. Read it over softly and easily, and you will hear that they have the very sound of sleep in them.

34

The Passionate Man's Pilgrimage, supposed to be written by one at the point of death

Give me my scallop-shell of quiet,
My staff of faith to walk upon,
My scrip of joy, immortal diet,
My bottle of salvation,
My gown of glory, hope's true gage,
And thus I'll take my pilgrimage.

Blood must be my body's balmer,
No other balm will there be given,
Whilst my soul like a white palmer
Travels to the land of heaven,
Over the silver mountains,
Where spring the nectar fountains ;
And there I'll kiss
The bowl of bliss,
And drink my everlasting fill
On every milken hill.
My soul will be a-dry before,
But after it will ne'er thirst more.

And by the happy blissful way
More peaceful pilgrims I shall see,

That have shook off their gowns of clay
And go apparelled fresh like me.
I'll bring them first
To slake their thirst,
And then to taste those nectar suckets,
At the clear wells
Where sweetness dwells,
Drawn up by saints in crystal buckets.

And when our bottles and all we
Are filled with immortality,
Then the holy paths we'll travel,
Strewed with rubies thick as gravel,
Ceilings of diamonds, sapphire floors,
High walls of coral and pearl bowers.

From thence to heaven's bribeless hall
Where no corrupted voices brawl,
No conscience molten into gold,
No forged accusers bought and sold,
No cause deferred, nor vain-spent journey,
For there Christ is the King's Attorney,
Who pleads for all without degrees,
And he hath angels, but no fees.

When the grand twelve million jury
Of our sins and direful fury
'Gainst our souls black verdicts give,
Christ pleads his death, and then we live.
Be thou my speaker, taintless pleader,
Unblotted lawyer, true proceeder ;
Thou movest salvation even for alms,
Not with a bribèd lawyer's palms.

And this is my eternal plea
To him that made heaven, earth, and sea :
Seeing my flesh must die so soon,
And want a head to dine next noon,
Just at the stroke when my veins start and spread,
Set on my soul an everlasting head.
Then am I ready, like a palmer fit,
To tread those blest paths which before I writ.

Scoloker's *Daiphantus*, 1604.   SIR WALTER RALEIGH.

Scallop-shell, the badge of a pilgrim.
Scrip, wallet.
Palmer, pilgrim.
Suckets, sweets.
Angels, a pun on angels of heaven, and the coins called angels, worth
    about 6s. 8d.

Sir Walter Raleigh, one of the greatest of Elizabethan adventurers
and courtiers, outlived his time ; there was no place for him when
James I decided on a policy of friendship with Spain. In 1603 a plot
against James was discovered, and the chief plotter accused Raleigh
of taking part in it. At Raleigh's trial, the King's Attorney brutally
cross-examined him, shouting, " Thou hast a Spanish heart, and thyself
art a viper from hell." The jury convicted him and he was condemned
to death. Later he was reprieved, and kept in prison until 1617, when
he was sent on a hopeless quest to South America, came back unsuc-
cessful, and was executed to please the Spaniards.

The poem was probably written just before his reprieve, while he
still thought he was doomed to death. The first part is peaceful and
resigned ; but gradually the bitter words creep in—corrupted, forged,
deferred, vain-spent ; and in " Not with a bribèd lawyer's palms "
we hear the ring of uncontrollable indignation.

35

Sister awake, close not your eyes,
  The day her light discloses,
And the bright morning doth arise
  Out of her bed of roses.

[59]

See the clear sun, the world's bright eye,
    In at our window peeping ;
Lo how he blusheth, to espy
    Us idle wenches sleeping.
Therefore awake, make haste I say,
    And let us without staying
All in our gowns of green so gay
    Into the park a-maying.

Bateson's *First Set of English*   ANONYMOUS.
    Madrigals, 1604.

There is a gramophone record of this madrigal.   One person begins
the singing and then the others follow.   The music becomes louder
and more impressive when the " clear sun " is mentioned, and quiet
and lazily drawn out with the words " idle wenches ".   " Therefore
awake " comes after a pause, very loudly and with all the voices
together ; and the last two lines are tripping and cheerful.

36

Fain would I change that note
    To which fond love hath charmed me,
Long, long to sing by rote,
    Fancying that that harmed me.
Yet when this thought doth come,
" Love is the perfect sum
    Of all delight,"
I have no other choice
Either for pen or voice
    To sing or write.

O love, they wrong thee much,
    That say thy sweet is bitter,
When thy riper fruit is such
    As nothing can be sweeter.

[60]

Fair house of joy and bliss,
Where truest pleasure is,
    I do adore thee ;
I know thee what thou art,
I serve thee with my heart
    And fall before thee.

Musical Humours, 1605.   TOBIAS HUME.

37

Fools, they are the only nation
Worth men's envy or admiration ;
Free from care or sorrow-taking ;
Themselves and others merry making :
All they speak or do is sterling.
Your fool he is your great man's darling,
And your ladies' sport and pleasure ;
Tongue and babble are his treasure.
Even his face begetteth laughter,
And he speaks truth, free from slaughter ;
He's the grace of every feast,
And, sometimes, the chiefest guest ;
Hath his trencher and his stool,
When wit shall wait upon the fool.
    O, who would not be
        He, he, he ?

Volpone ; or, The Fox.   BEN JONSON.

" Free from slaughter " seems to be put instead of " free from
slander ", simply for the sake of the rhyme. The whole poem should
be read rather quickly, working up to the gay laughter of " he, he,
he ".

There is a garden in her face
Where roses and white lilies grow ;
A heavenly paradise is that place
Wherein all pleasant fruits do flow.
    There cherries grow which none may buy,
    Till Cherry-ripe themselves do cry.

Those cherries fairly do enclose
Of orient pearl a double row,
Which when her lovely laughter shows,
They look like rose-buds filled with snow ;
    Yet them nor peer nor prince can buy,
    Till Cherry-ripe themselves do cry.

Her eyes like angels watch them still ;
Her brows like bended bows do stand,
Threatening with piercing frowns to kill
All that attempt with eye or hand
    Those sacred cherries to come nigh
    Till Cherry-ripe themselves do cry.

Alison's *An Hour's Recreation*   THOMAS CAMPION.
in Music, 1606.

This is a clever use of what after all was, to Campion and his friends,
a very ordinary street cry ; one with no more interest to them than
those that Ben Jonson gives about this time in his play *Bartholomew
Fair*—
        A number of people pass over the stage
    LEATHERHEAD *the toy-seller* (*sitting by his wares*). What d'you
lack ? What is't you buy ? What d'you lack ? Rattles, drums,
halberts, horses, babies o' the best, fiddles of the finest ?
    COSTARD-MONGER. Buy any pears, pears, fine, very fine pears !
    JOAN TRASH. Buy any gingerbread, gilt gingerbread !
    NIGHTINGALE (*selling ballads*). Hey,
                Now the Fair's a-filling !
                O for a tune to startle

The birds o' the booths here billing,
Yearly with old Saint Bartle !
Buy any ballads, new ballads ?

39

Enter an old shepherd, with a bell ringing, and the Priest of Pan following.

PRIEST. Shepherds all, and maidens fair,
Fold your flocks up, for the air
'Gins to thicken, and the sun
Already his great course hath run.
See the dew-drops how they kiss
Every little flower that is,
Hanging on their velvet heads,
Like a rope of crystal beads.
See the heavy clouds low falling,
And bright Hesperus down calling
The dead Night from under ground,
At whose rising, mists unsound,
Damps and vapours fly apace,
Hovering o'er the wanton face
Of these pastures, where they come,
Striking dead both bud and bloom.
Therefore from such danger lock
Everyone his loved flock,
And let your dogs lie loose without,
Lest the wolf come as a scout
From the mountain, and ere day
Bear a lamb or kid away ;
Or the crafty thievish fox
Break upon your simple flocks.
To secure yourselves from these,
Be not too secure in ease ;

[63]

Let one eye his watches keep,
Whilst the t'other eye doth sleep ;
So you shall good shepherds prove,
And for ever hold the love
Of our great god.   Sweetest slumbers
And soft silence fall in numbers
On your eyelids ; so farewell,
Thus I end my evening's knell.

The Faithful Shepherdess.   JOHN FLETCHER.

40

All ye woods, and trees and bowers,
All ye virtues and ye powers
That inhabit in the lakes,
In the pleasant springs or brakes,
    Move your feet
    To our sound,
    Whilst we greet
    All this ground
With his honour and his name,
That defends our flocks from blame.

He is great, and he is just,
He is ever good, and must
Thus be honoured : daffodillies,
Roses, pinks, and lovèd lilies
    Let us fling,
    Whilst we sing,
    Ever holy,
    Ever holy,
Ever honoured ever young,
Thus great Pan is ever sung.

The Faithful Shepherdess.   JOHN FLETCHER.

41

Fear no more the heat o' the sun,
   Nor the furious winter's rages.
Thou thy worldly task hast done,
   Home art gone, and ta'en thy wages.
Golden lads and girls all must,
As chimney-sweepers, come to dust.

Fear no more the frown o' the great,
   Thou art past the tyrant's stroke ;
Care no more to clothe and eat,
   To thee the reed is as the oak.
The sceptre, learning, physic, must
All follow this, and come to dust.

Fear no more the lightning-flash,
   Nor the all-dreaded thunder-stone ;
Fear not slander, censure rash ;
   Thou hast finished joy and moan.
All lovers young, all lovers must
Consign to thee, and come to dust.

No exorciser harm thee,
Nor no witchcraft charm thee !
Ghost unlaid forbear thee !
Nothing ill come near thee !
Quiet consummation have,
And renownèd be thy grave !

Cymbeline, 1609–10.   WILLIAM SHAKESPEARE.

Exorciser, a person who has power over ghosts and spirits.
Ghost unlaid, a ghost which is still wandering, and has not been exorcised
   or made to rest.

A Religious Use of Taking Tobacco

The Indian weed witherèd quite,
Green at morn, cut down at night,
Shows thy decay all flesh is hay ;
    Thus think, then drink tobacco.

And when the smoke ascends on high
Think thou beholdst the vanity
Of worldly stuff, gone with a puff ;
    Thus think, then drink tobacco.

But when the pipe grows foul within,
Think of thy soul defiled with sin
And that the fire doth it require ;
    Thus think, then drink tobacco.

The ashes that are left behind
May serve to put thee still in mind
That into dust return thou must ;
    Thus think, then drink tobacco.

ANONYMOUS.

There are many references, from 1580 onwards, to the taking or
drinking of tobacco. There are accounts by travellers in Virginia,
telling how the Indians " use to take the fume or smoke thereof by
sucking it through pipes made of clay " ; and there are protests like
that of the Citizen's Wife in *The Knight of the Burning Pestle* : " Now,
I pray, gentlemen, what good does this stinking tobacco do you ?
Nothing, I warrant you ; make chimneys of your faces ! " But this
poem, from a manuscript now in Dublin, is unusual in making a sermon
out of the habit.

The sea hath many thousand sands,
The sun hath motes as many,
The sky is full of stars, and love
As full of woes as any.
Believe me, that do know the elf,
And make no trial by thyself.

It is in truth a pretty toy
For babes to play withal ;
But O the honeys of our youth
Are oft our age's gall !
Self-proof in time will make thee know
He was a prophet told thee so :

A prophet that, Cassandra-like,
Tells truth without belief,
For headstrong youth will run his race,
Although his goal be grief ;
Love's martyr, when his heat is past,
Proves Care's confessor at the last.

Jones' *Muses' Garden for Delights*, 1610.   ANONYMOUS.

Motes, spots.
Elf, mischievous creature.
Gall, bitterness.
Cassandra, daughter of King Priam of Troy. She was gifted with the
    power of always prophesying the truth ; but doomed never to be
    believed.
Love's martyr, etc., he who when young is in love will, as he grows
    older, have nothing but cares to think about.

There is only one known copy in the world of Jones' *Muses' Garden
for Delights* ; it was bought by an American in 1917, and is now in
New York.

44

Lay a garland on my hearse
    Of the dismal yew ;
Maidens, willow branches bear ;
    Say, I died true.

My love was false, but I was firm
    From my hour of birth ;
Upon my buried body lie
    Lightly, gentle earth.

The Maid's Tragedy, 1611.   FRANCIS BEAUMONT
                                       and JOHN FLETCHER.

45

Let not the sluggish sleep
    Close up thy waking eye,
Until with judgment deep
    Thy daily deeds thou try.

He that one sin in conscience keeps,
    When he to quiet goes,
More venturous is than he that sleeps
    With twenty mortal foes.

Byrd's *Psalms, Songs, and Sonnets*, 1611.   ANONYMOUS.

46. A Bellman's Song

Maids to bed, and cover coal,
Let the mouse out of her hole ;

[68]

Crickets in the chimney sing
Whilst the little bell doth ring.
If fast asleep, who can tell
When the clapper hits the bell?

Ravenscroft's *Melismata*, 1611. THOMAS CAMPION.

Clapper, the tongue of the bell.

47

Full fathom five thy father lies,
Of his bones are coral made;
Those are pearls that were his eyes:
Nothing of him that doth fade
But doth suffer a sea-change
Into something rich and strange.
Sea nymphs hourly ring his knell. [*Ding-dong*.
Hark! now I hear them,
Ding-dong, bell!

The Tempest, 1611–12. WILLIAM SHAKESPEARE.

"Where should this music be? In the air, or the earth?
It sounds no more; and sure, it waits upon
Some god of the island. Sitting on a bank,
Weeping again the king my father's wreck,
This music crept by me upon the waters,
Allaying both their fury and my passion,
With its sweet air."
And, as the prince Ferdinand says when the magic songs have
died away,
"The ditty does remember my drowned father.
This is no mortal business, nor no sound
That the earth owns."

Call for the robin-redbreast and the wren,
Since o'er shady groves they hover,
And with leaves and flowers do cover
The friendless bodies of unburied men.
Call unto his funeral dole
The ant, the fieldmouse, and the mole,
To rear him hillocks that shall keep him warm,
And (when gay tombs are robbed) sustain no harm ;
But keep the wolf far thence, that's foe to men,
For with his nails he'll dig them up again.

The White Devil, 1612.   JOHN WEBSTER.

Dole, mourning.

" I never saw anything like this dirge," said Charles Lamb, " except
the ditty which reminds Ferdinand of his drowned father in *The
Tempest*. As that is of the water, watery ; so this is of the earth,
earthy."

Epitaph on Salathiel Pavy, a Child of Queen Elizabeth's Chapel

Weep with me all you that read
    This little story,
And know, for whom a tear you shed,
    Death's self is sorry.
'Twas a child that so did thrive
    In grace, and feature,
As heaven and nature seemed to strive
    Which owned the creature.
Years he numbered scarce thirteen
    When fates turned cruel,

Yet three filled zodiacs had he been
    The stage's jewel ;
And did act (what now we moan)
    Old men so duly,
As, sooth, the Parcae thought him one,
    He played so truly.
So, by error, to his fate
    They all consented ;
But viewing him since (alas, too late)
    They have repented,
And have sought (to give new birth)
    In baths to steep him ;
But, being so much too good for earth,
    Heaven vows to keep him.

Epigrams.   BEN JONSON.

Zodiacs, years.
Parcae, the fates.
In baths to steep him, like the daughters of the old king Pelias, in the
    Greek story. They were persuaded by the enchantress Medea
    to cut their father to pieces, and put him into a cauldron, so that
    he might be made young again. But they found to their horror
    that it was all a trick.

Salathiel Pavy evidently belonged to a company of boy actors,
who were very popular in London in the early years of King James's
reign. There were no women actors at this time, and so the women
in the plays had all to be acted by boys.

50

What is our life ?   A play of passion,
Our mirth the music of division.
Our mothers' wombs the tiring-houses be,
Where we are dressed for this short comedy.
Heaven the judicious sharp spectator is,
That sits and marks still who doth act amiss.

[71]

Our graves that hide us from the searching sun
Are like drawn curtains when the play is done.
Thus march we, playing, to our latest rest ;
Only we die in earnest, that's no jest.

Gibbons, *First Set of Madrigals*   Sir Walter Raleigh.
   and Mottets, 1612.

Tiring-houses, dressing-rooms.

If you know the famous speech in Shakespeare's *As You Like It* (Act II, scene 7), beginning " All the world's a stage ", compare it with this poem. Raleigh here is not trying to describe the scenes in his comedy of life, as Shakespeare does, but only to point out the comparison. But perhaps, he ends up, life is not a comedy after all, for its ending must be tragic.

51

Roses, their sharp spines being gone,   [*M*
Not royal in their smells alone,
   But in their hue ;
Maiden pinks, of odour faint,
Daisies smell-less, yet most quaint,
   And sweet thyme true ;

Primrose, firstborn child of Ver,
Merry springtime's harbinger,
   With harebells dim ;
Oxlips in their cradles growing,
Marigolds on death-beds blowing,
   Larks'-heels trim :

All dear Nature's children sweet
Lie 'fore bride and bridegroom's feet,   [*Strew flou*
   Blessing their sense.

[72]

Not an angel of the air,
Bird melodious or bird fair,
    Is absent hence.

The crow, the slanderous cuckoo, nor
The boding raven, nor chough hoar,
    Nor chattering pie,
May on our bride-house perch or sing,
Or with them any discord bring,
    But from it fly.

Two Noble Kinsmen, 1612–13.   WILLIAM SHAKESPEARE
                                        and JOHN FLETCHER.

Hymen, god of marriage.
Ver, spring.
Hoar, white.

52

Jack and Joan they think no ill,
But loving live, and merry still ;
Do their week-days' work, and pray
Devoutly on the holy day ;
Skip and trip it on the green,
And help to choose the Summer Queen ;
Lash out at a country feast
Their silver penny with the best.

Well can they judge of nappy ale,
And tell at large a winter tale ;
Climb up to the apple loft,
And turn the crabs till they be soft.
Tib is all the father's joy,
And little Tom the mother's boy.

[73]

All their pleasure is content,
And care, to pay their yearly rent.

Joan can call by name her cows,
And deck her windows with green boughs.
She can wreaths and tutties make,
And trim with plums a bridal cake.
Jack knows what brings gain or loss,
And his long flail can stoutly toss,
Make the hedge which others break,
And ever thinks what he doth speak.

Now you courtly dames and knights,
That study only strange delights,
Though you scorn the home-spun gray
And revel in your rich array,
Though your tongues dissemble deep,
And can your heads from danger keep ;
Yet for all your pomp and train,
Securer lives the silly swain.

First Book of Airs, 1613.   THOMAS CAMPION.

Nappy, foaming, strong.
Tutties, nosegays.
Homespun, cloth made at home.

  Notice the details about life in the country, and the cleverly chosen
phrases, such as " tell *at large* a winter tale " (rambling on with it),
" make the hedge which *others* break " (the courtly dames and knights,
in their hunting perhaps), and " *strange* delights " (far-fetched ones,
because they get so quickly bored with the ordinary pleasures).

53

Now winter nights enlarge
  The number of their hours,

And clouds their storms discharge
  Upon the airy towers.
Now let the chimneys blaze,
  And cups o'erflow with wine ;
Let well-tuned words amaze
  With harmony divine.
Now yellow waxen lights
  Shall wait on honey love,
While youthful revels, masques, and courtly sights
  Sleep's leaden spells remove.

This time doth well dispense
  With lovers' long discourse ;
Much speech hath some defence,
  Though beauty no remorse.
All do not all things well :
  Some measures comely tread,
Some knotted riddles tell,
  Some poems smoothly read.
The summer hath his joys
  And winter his delights ;
Though love and all his pleasures are but toys,
  They shorten tedious nights.

Third Book of Airs, 1617.   THOMAS CAMPION.

Measures, dances.

The last poem described the villagers' life ; here is the scene in a
big country house in winter, with the firelight and candlelight, and
all the ways of filling up the long evenings.

54

To his sweet lute Apollo sung the motions of the spheres,
The wondrous order of the stars, whose course divides
    the years,

[75]

And all the mysteries above,
But none of this could Midas move,
Which purchased him his ass's ears.

Then Pan with his rude pipe began the country-wealth
    to advance ;
To boast of cattle, flocks of sheep, and goats on hills that
    dance,
        With much more of this childish kind,
        That quite transported Midas' mind,
        And held him wrapped as in a trance.

This wrong the God of Music scorned from such a
    sottish judge,
And bent his angry bow at Pan, which made the piper
    trudge ;
        Then Midas' head he so did trim,
        That every age yet talks of him
        And Phoebus' right-revengèd grudge.

Fourth Book of Airs, 1617.   THOMAS CAMPION.

Apollo was the glorious god of the sun, of beauty, and of all sweet
singing ; and Pan was the friendly god of the fields, of flocks and of
shepherds. Midas was too dull to understand the music of Apollo,
and was punished with a pair of ass's ears, which he tried to hide, but
the secret came out in the end.

The poem does not try to point any moral ; it just tells, with music
that fits the words, a story that everyone knew. But the moral is
clear if one wants it.

55

Arm, arm, arm, arm ! the scouts are all come in ;
Keep your ranks close, and now your honours win.

Behold from yonder hill the foe appears ;
Bows, bills, glaives, arrows, shields, and spears !
Like a dark wood he comes, or tempest pouring ;
O view the wings of horse the meadows scouring.
The van-guard marches bravely. Hark, the drums ! [*Dub, dub.*
They meet, they meet, and now the battle comes :
    See how the arrows fly
    That darken all the sky !
    Hark how the trumpets sound,
    Hark how the hills rebound,   [*Tara, tara, tara, tara, tara.*
Hark how the horses charge ! in, boys, boys, in !
The battle totters ; now the wounds begin :
    O how they cry !
    O how they die !
Room for the valiant Memnon, armed with thunder,
  See how he breaks the ranks asunder !
They fly ! They fly ! Eumenes has the chase,
And brave Polybius makes good his place.
    To the plains, to the woods,
    To the rocks, to the floods,
They fly for succour. Follow, follow, follow !
Hark how the soldiers hollo !   [*Hey, hey.*
    Brave Diocles is dead,
    And all his soldiers fled ;
    The battle's won, and lost,
    That many a life hath cost.

The Mad Lover.   JOHN FLETCHER.

Glaives, broadswords.
Hollo, shout.

Memnon, the chief character in the play, imagines that he sees the
ghost of his old enemy Diocles, whom he had conquered. He says,
        " Sing me the battle of Pelusium,
         In which this worthy died,"
and the song follows, with the sounds of the drums and trumpets, and
the shouts of the victorious soldiers, coming in as accompaniment.

It should be recited with plenty of speed and spirit ; the sounds of the
accompaniment beginning softly, growing louder and quickly fading
away.   And so
> " The battle's won, and lost,
>   That many a life hath cost."

56

Sweet Suffolk owl, so trimly dight
  With feathers, like a lady bright,
Thou sing'st alone, sitting by night,
    Te whit, te whoo !

Thy note that forth so freely rolls
  With shrill command the mouse controls,
And sings a dirge for dying souls,
    Te whit, te whoo !

Songs of Divers Airs and Natures, 1619.   THOMAS VAUTOR.

57

To see a strange outlandish fowl,
A quaint baboon, an ape, an owl,
A dancing bear, a giant's bone,
A foolish engine move alone,
A morris-dance, a puppet play,
Mad Tom to sing a roundelay,
A woman dancing on a rope ;
Bull-baiting also at *The Hope* ;
A rhymer's jests, a juggler's cheats,
A tumbler showing cunning feats,
Or players acting on the stage,
There goes the bounty of our age :

But unto any pious motion,
There's little coin, and less devotion.

St. Paul's Church, her Bill for the   HENRY FARLEY.
Parliament, 1621.

This song comes from a most curious book, an appeal spoken by
the church of St. Paul's in London, for money to repair and rebuild
it. The appeal had its effect, for James I began the repairing, and
Charles I continued it, partly at his own expense. But the Great Fire
of 1666 utterly destroyed the whole cathedral.

The song tells us much about the interests and amusements of the
townspeople. Some of them are ordinary entertainments, such as
dancing, singing, juggling, acting, Punch and Judy; some are wonders,
such as strange animals and birds and fossils.

The " foolish engine " was a perpetual motion machine, made by
an inventor called Cornelis Drebbel. He also claimed to have in-
vented magic lanterns and submarines, and to have introduced into
England the microscope, telescope, and thermometer.

Would such a poem as this have any point nowadays? What
kind of entertainments would it mention?

58

I

The faery beam upon you,
The stars to glister on you;
    A moon of light
    In the noon of night,
Till the fire-drake hath o'ergone you!

The wheel of fortune guide you,
The boy with the bow beside you;
    Run aye in the way
    Till the bird of day,
And the luckier lot betide you!

[79]

To the old, long life and treasure,
To the young, all health and pleasure ;
    To the fair, their face
    With eternal grace,
And the foul to be loved at leisure !

To the witty, all clear mirrors,
To the foolish, their dark errors ;
    To the loving sprite,
    A secure delight,
To the jealous, his own false terrors !

The Masque of the Gypsies, 1621.   BEN JONSON.

Foul, plain, ugly.
Sprite, spirit, person.

The first of these songs is the gipsy's wish of good luck ; the second is a series of wishes, good and bad, to fit different types of people.

59. A Christmas Carol

So, now is come our joyful'st feast ;
Let every man be jolly.
Each room with ivy leaves is dressed,
And every post with holly.
    Though some churls at our mirth repine,
    Round your foreheads garlands twine,
    Drown sorrow in a cup of wine,
And let us all be merry.

Now, all our neighbours' chimneys smoke,
And Christmas blocks are burning ;
Their ovens they with baked-meats choke,
And all their spits are turning.

Without the door, let sorrow lie :
And if for cold it hap to die,
We'll bury it in a Christmas pie,
And evermore be merry.

Now, every lad is wondrous trim,
And no man minds his labour.
Our lasses have provided them
A bag-pipe and a tabor.
   Young men, and maids, and girls and boys,
   Give life to one another's joys ;
   And you anon shall by their noise
Perceive that they are merry.

Rank misers now do sparing shun,
Their hall of music soundeth ;
And dogs thence with whole shoulders run,
So all things there aboundeth.
   The country-folk themselves advance,
   For Crowdy-mutton's come out of France ;
   And Jack shall pipe, and Jill shall dance,
And all the town be merry.

Ned Swash hath fetched his bands from pawn,
And all his best apparel.
Brisk Nell hath bought a ruff of lawn,
With droppings of the barrel.
   And those that hardly all the year
   Had bread to eat, or rags to wear,
   Will have both clothes and dainty fare,
And all the day be merry.

Now poor men to the justices
With capons make their arrants,

F

And if they hap to fail of these,
They plague them with their warrants.
  But now they feed them with good cheer,
  And what they want, they take in beer :
  For, *Christmas comes but once a year* ;
And then they shall be merry.

Good farmers, in the country, nurse
The poor, that else were undone.
Some landlords spend their money worse
On lust, and pride at London.
  There the roysters they do play,
  Drab and dice their lands away,
  Which may be ours another day ;
And therefore let's be merry.

The client now his suit forbears,
The prisoner's heart is easèd.
The debtor drinks away his cares,
And for the time is pleasèd.
  Though others' purses be more fat,
  Why should we pine or grieve at that ?
  Hang sorrow, care will kill a cat,
And therefore let's be merry.

Hark, how the wags abroad do call
Each other forth to rambling.
Anon you'll see them in the hall,
For nuts and apples scrambling.
  Hark, how the roofs with laughter sound !
  Anon they'll think the house goes round ;
  For they the cellar's depth have found,
And there they will be merry.

The wenches with their wassail-bowls
About the streets are singing ;

The boys are come to catch the owls,
The wild-mare in is bringing.
  Our kitchen-boy hath broke his box,
  And to the dealing of the ox
  Our honest neighbours come in flocks,
And here they will be merry.

Now kings and queens poor sheepcotes have,
And mate with everybody ;
The honest, now, may play the knave,
And wise men play at Noddy.
  Some youths will now a-mumming go ;
  Some others play at Rowland-ho,
  And twenty other gambols mo,
Because they will be merry.

Then wherefore in these merry days
Should we I pray be duller ?
No, let us sing some roundelays,
To make our mirth the fuller.
  And whilest thus inspired we sing,
  Let all the streets with echoes ring ;
  Woods, and hills, and everything,
Bear witness we are merry.

A Miscellany of Epigrams, 1622.   GEORGE WITHER.

Crowdy-mutton, a French fiddler.
Ruff of lawn, a ruff made of fine linen.
Capons, chickens.
Arrants, errands.
Roysters, revellers.
Wild-mare, " shoeing the wild-mare " was a children's Christmas game.
Dealing of the ox, dividing the roasted ox among the poorer neighbours.
Noddy, a card-game (with a pun on noddy, a fool).
Mumming, acting in Christmas plays.
Rowland-ho, some kind of game. This is the only mention of it.

60

Sweet was the song the Virgin sung,
    When she to Bethlehem was come,
And was delivered of her Son,
    That blessed Jesus hath to name.
Sweet Babe, quoth she, lull-lullaby,
    My Son and eke a Saviour born,
Who hath vouchsafèd from on high
    To visit us that were forlorn.
Lull-lullaby sweet Babe, sang she,
    And sweetly rocked him on her knee.

Attey's *First Book of Airs*, 1622.   ANONYMOUS.

Attey's *Book of Airs* has the words printed beneath each line of music. In this song, because the words have to fit the music, lulla lullaby is repeated many times ; and the last line runs, " And sweetly rocked him, rocked him, and sweetly rocked him, and sweetly, sweetly, sweetly rocked him on her knee." With repetitions like this it is sometimes almost impossible to reconstruct the original poem.

61

Epitaph on the Countess Dowager of Pembroke

Underneath this marble hearse
Lies the subject of all verse,
Sidney's sister, Pembroke's mother ;
Death, ere thou hast killed another,
Fair, and learn'd, and good as she,
Time shall throw a dart at thee.

Camden's *Remains concerning*   WILLIAM BROWNE.
Britain, 1623.

Sir Philip Sidney dedicated his chief book to his sister, the Countess of Pembroke, who was the centre of a distinguished group of writers.

Her son, the third Earl of Pembroke, was a friend and patron of Shakespeare and Donne, and, among many other things, organized an expedition to Virginia. The writers helped and befriended by the family are innumerable ; so the Countess of Pembroke was indeed worthy to be the " subject of verse ".

62

This world a hunting is,
The prey poor man, the Nimrod fierce is Death,
His speedy greyhounds are
Lust, sickness, envy, care,
Strife that ne'er falls amiss,
With all those ills which haunt us while we breathe.
Now if (by chance) we fly
Of these the eager chase,
Old age with stealing pace
Casts up his nets, and there we panting die.

Flowers of Sion.   WILLIAM DRUMMOND.

Nimrod, huntsman.

63

Hark, now everything is still—
The screech-owl, and the whistler shrill,
Call upon our dame, aloud,
And bid her quickly don her shroud :
Much you had of land and rent,
Your length in clay's now competent.
A long war disturbed your mind,
Here your perfect peace is signed.

Of what is't fools make such vain keeping?
Sin their conception, their birth, weeping:
Their life, a general mist of error,
Their death, a hideous storm of terror.
Strew your hair with powders sweet;
Don clean linen, bathe your feet,
And (the foul fiend more to check)
A crucifix let bless your neck.
'Tis now full tide, 'tween night, and day,
End your groan, and come away.

The Duchess of Malfi, 1623.   JOHN WEBSTER.

Competent, enough for you.
'Tis now full tide, the time is up.

64. A Hymn to God the Father

Wilt thou forgive that sin, where I begun,
  Which is my sin, though it were done before?
Wilt thou forgive those sins through which I run
  And do run still, though still I do deplore?
    When thou hast done, thou hast not done,
      For I have more.

Wilt thou forgive that sin, by which I have won
  Others to sin, and made my sin their door?
Wilt thou forgive that sin which I did shun
  A year or two, but wallowed in, a score?
    When thou hast done, thou hast not done,
      For I have more.

I have a sin of fear, that when I have spun
  My last thread I shall perish on the shore;

Swear by thyself that at my death thy son
   Shall shine as he shines now, and heretofore ;
    And having done that, thou hast done,
      I fear no more.

Poems.   JOHN DONNE.

John Donne, who wrote *The Triple Fool* (No. 16), had a gay and adventurous youth, but in 1615 took orders and later became Dean of St. Paul's. There he repaired and beautified the building (see note on No. 57), and preached some of the finest sermons in English literature. His later poems, full of repentance for his early life, still keep the harsh and vivid conversational rhythm that there was in *The Triple Fool.*

This hymn was probably written at a time when he was very seriously ill, in 1623 ; it was later set to " a most grave and solemn tune ", and often sung by the choristers of St. Paul's.

Notice the pun on the word Son in the last verse. There may also be a pun on his own name in the ending of each verse, for Donne was pronounced Dun ; so that the last two lines of the first verse may mean, " When God had forgiven his sins, He still did not possess Donne, for there were many more sins to forgive."

65

Haymakers, rakers, reapers, and mowers,
   Wait on your Summer Queen ;
Dress up with musk-rose her eglantine bowers,
   Daffodils strew the green.
       Sing, dance, and play,
       'Tis holiday ;
The sun does bravely shine
   On our ears of corn.
     Rich as a pearl
     Comes every girl ;
This is mine, this is mine, this is mine ;
   Let us die, ere away they be borne.

Bow to the Sun, to our Queen, and that fair one
  Come to behold our sports.
Each bonny lass here is counted a rare one
  As those in princes' courts.
        These and we
        With country glee
  Will teach the woods to resound,
    And the hills with echo's hollo.
        Skipping lambs
        Their bleating dams
  'Mongst kids shall trip it round;
    For joy thus our wenches we follow.

Wind, jolly huntsmen, your neat bugles shrilly,
  Hounds make a lusty cry;
Spring up, you falconers, the partridges freely,
  Then let your brave hawks fly.
        Horses amain
        Over ridge over plain;
  The dogs have the stag in chase.
    'Tis a sport to content a king.
        So ho ho! through the skies
        How the proud bird flies,
  And sousing kills with a grace!
    Now the deer falls. Hark, how they ring!

The Sun's Darling.   THOMAS DEKKER.

Sousing, swooping, pouncing.

66

Hence all you vain delights,
As short as are the nights,
Wherein you spend your folly,

There's nought in this life sweet,
If man were wise to see't,
  But only melancholy,
  O sweetest melancholy.
Welcome folded arms, and fixèd eyes,
A sigh that piercing mortifies,
A look that's fastened to the ground,
A tongue chained up without a sound.

Fountain heads, and pathless groves,
Places which pale passion loves ;
Moon-light walks, when all the fowls
Are warmly housed, save bats and owls ;
  A mid-night bell, a parting groan,
  These are the sounds we feed upon ;
Then stretch our bones in a still gloomy valley,
Nothing's so dainty sweet, as lovely melancholy.

The Nice Valour.   JOHN FLETCHER.

67

A Proper New Ballad, entitled The Fairies' Farewell or God-a-Mercy Will ; to be sung or whistled to the tune of the Meadow Brow by the learned ; by the unlearned, to the tune of Fortune

" Farewell rewards and fairies,"
  Good housewives now may say,
For now foul sluts in dairies
  Do fare as well as they ;
And though they sweep their hearths no less
  Than maids were wont to do,
Yet who of late for cleanliness
  Finds sixpence in her shoe ?

Lament, lament old abbeys,
  The fairies' lost command,
They did but change priests' babies,
  But some have changed your land;
And all your children stol'n from thence
  Are now grown puritans,
Who live as changelings ever since
  For love of your domains.

At morning and at evening both,
  You merry were and glad;
So little care of sleep and sloth
  These pretty ladies had,
When Tom came home from labour,
  Or Ciss to milking rose;
Then merrily went their tabor,
  And nimbly went their toes.

Witness those rings and roundelays
  Of theirs which yet remain,
Were footed in Queen Mary's days
  On many a grassy plain.
But since of late Elizabeth
  And later James came in,
They never danced on any heath
  As when the time had been.

By which we note the fairies
  Were of the old profession,
Their songs were *Ave Maries*,
  Their dances were procession;
But now alas they all are dead
  Or gone beyond the seas,
Or further for religion fled,
  Or else they take their ease.

A tell-tale in their company
  They never could endure,
And whoso kept not secretly
  Their mirth, was punished sure.
It was a just and Christian deed
  To pinch such black and blue ;
O how the commonwealth doth need
  Such justices as you !

Now they have left our quarters,
  A register they have,
Who can preserve their charters,
  A man both wise and grave.
A hundred of their merry pranks,
  By one that I could name
Are kept in store ; con twenty thanks
  To William for the same.

To William Churne of Staffordshire
  Give laud and praises due ;
Who every meal can mend your cheer
  With tales both old and true.
To William all give audience,
  And pray you for his noddle ;
For all the fairies' evidence
  Were lost if it were addle.

Certain Elegant Poems.   Bishop Corbet.

Ave Maries, prayers to the Virgin Mary.
  Shakespeare's comedies are full of talk about fairies, from Titania
and Oberon in *A Midsummer Night's Dream*, and those pretended ones
that attack the wicked jolly Falstaff in *The Merry Wives of Windsor*,
and
    " Pinch him and burn him and turn him about,
      Till candles and starlight and moonshine be out ",
to the tricksy spirit Ariel in *The Tempest*, who sings the song " Full
fathom five " (No. 47). So they did not entirely fade away when

Roman Catholic gave way to Protestant ; but Puritans had little use for such ideas, and only men like Corbet, who though Bishop of Oxford had not the Puritan sternness and strictness, were left to regret the disappearance of the fairies.

68. Hymn

All this night shrill chanticler,
Day's proclaiming trumpeter,
Claps his wings and loudly cries :
" Mortals ! mortals ! wake and rise !
    See a wonder,
    Heaven is under ;
From the earth is risse a sun
Shines all night, though day be done.

" Wake, O earth ! wake, every thing !
Wake, and hear the joy I bring ;
Wake and joy, for all this night
Heaven and every twinkling light
    All amazing
    Still stand gazing ;
Angels, powers, and all that be,
Wake, and joy this sun to see."

Hail, O sun ! O blessed light
Sent into the world by night !
Let thy rays and heavenly powers
Shine in this dark soul of ours,
    For most duly
    Thou art truly
God and man, we do confess :
Hail, O Sun of Righteousness !

Certain Divine Carols, 1626.   WILLIAM AUSTIN.

Fly hence, shadows, that do keep
Watchful sorrows charmed in sleep !
Though the eyes be overtaken,
Yet the heart doth ever waken
Thoughts, chained up in busy snares
Of continual woes and cares :
Love and griefs are so expressed
As they rather sigh than rest.
Fly hence, shadows, that do keep
Watchful sorrows charmed in sleep !

The Lover's Melancholy, 1629.   JOHN FORD.

This is a gentle awakening song ; in the play Melander has lost
his daughter, and is mad with grief. He is given a potion, and sleeps,
and is awakened by this song to find that his daughter is safe. The
words show that his is no restful sleep : though his eyes are closed
his heart is full of care and grief that prevent rest. Then let him
waken, and find his happiness.

70

A rose, as fair as ever saw the north,
Grew in a little garden all alone ;
A sweeter flower did Nature ne'er put forth,
Nor fairer garden yet was never known ;
The maidens danced about it morn and noon,
And learned bards of it their ditties made ;
The nimble fairies by the pale-faced moon
Watered the root and kissed her pretty shade.

But well-a-day, the gardener careless grew ;
The maids and fairies both were kept away,

And in a drought the caterpillars threw
Themselves upon the bud and every spray.

God shield the stock ! if heaven sends no supplies,
The fairest blossom of the garden dies.

WILLIAM BROWNE.

Though this is a sonnet in shape, the subject is much more simple
and straightforward than is usual in sonnets. It is found in a manu-
script beautifully written by some lover of poetry, who had also liked
and troubled to copy out Nos. 7, 50, and 61 in this book.

71. In Praise of Ale

Whenas the chill Charocco blows
   And winter tells a heavy tale,
When pies and daws and rooks and crows
Sit cursing of the frost and snows,
     Then give me ale.

Ale in a Saxon rumkin then,
   Such as will make grim Malkin prate,
Rouseth up valour in all men,
Quickens the poet's wit and pen,
     Despiseth fate.

Ale that the absent battle fights,
   And scorns the march of Swedish drum ;
Disputes the prince's laws and rights ;
And what is past tells mortal wights,
     And what's to come.

Ale, that the ploughman's heart up keeps
  And equals it with tyrants' thrones ;
That wipes the eyes that fain would weep,
And lulls in sweet and dainty sleep
        His wearied bones.

Grandchild of Ceres, barley's daughter,
  Wine's emulous neighbour, if but stale,
Ennobling all the nymphs of water
And filling each man's heart with laughter—
        Ha, ha, give me ale !

Wit and Drollery.   THOMAS BONHAM.

Pies, magpies.
Rumkin, drinking-glass.
Malkin, Mary.
Ceres, goddess of corn.

No one has been able to find out what the Charocco is, and even
the early editors were puzzled, and tried to alter it. Versions of it
are—" the Chilche Rocko blows ", " the Chilly Rock once blows ",
" the chill Sirocco blows " (but the Sirocco is an unpleasantly hot
wind).

" The Swedish drum " gives us a date for the poem, for in 1626–9
Gustavus Adolphus of Sweden was waging brilliant campaigns against
the Catholics in Germany.

72. Hos ego versiculos

Like to the damask rose you see,
Or like the blossom on the tree,
Or like the dainty flower of May,
Or like the morning to the day,
Or like the sun, or like the shade,
Or like the gourd which Jonas had ;
  Even such is man whose thread is spun,
  Drawn out and cut, and so is done.

[95]

The rose withers, the blossom blasteth,
The flower fades, the morning hasteth ;
The sun sets, the shadow flies,
The gourd consumes, and man he dies.

Like to the blaze of fond delight ;
Or like a morning clear and bright ;
Or like a frost, or like a shower,
Or like the pride of Babel's tower,
Or like the hour that guides the time,
Or like to beauty in her prime ;
   Even such is man, whose glory lends
   His life a blaze or two, and ends.

Delights vanish ; the morn o'ercasteth,
The frost breaks, the shower hasteth,
The tower falls, the hour spends ;
The beauty fades, and man's life ends.

Argalus and Parthenia, 1629.   FRANCIS QUARLES.

Hos ego versiculos . . . , I have made these verses . . .

This exercise in similes was most popular in the seventeenth century.
It was evidently a great temptation to try one's hand at it, for over
half a dozen authors have it printed in their works, with extra lines or
in different versions. Notice the way in which each simile is caught
up again, and given extra point, in the two four-line verses.

73. The Quip

The merry world did on a day
   With his train-bands and mates agree
To meet together, where I lay,
   And all in sport to jeer at me.

[96]

First, Beauty crept into a rose,
  Which when I plucked not, " Sir," said she,
" Tell me, I pray, whose hands are those?"
  But thou shalt answer, Lord, for me.

Then Money came, and chinking still,
  " What tune is this, poor man?" said he,
" I heard in music you had skill."
  But thou shalt answer, Lord, for me.

Then came brave Glory puffing by
  In silks that whistled, who but he?
He scarce allowed me half an eye.
  But thou shalt answer, Lord, for me.

Then came quick Wit and Conversation,
  And he would needs a comfort be,
And, to be short, make an oration.
  But thou shalt answer, Lord, for me.

Yet when the hour of thy design
  To answer these fine things shall come,
Speak not at large, say, I am thine ;
  And then they have their answer home.

The Temple, 1633.   GEORGE HERBERT.

Train-bands, citizen-soldiers.
Who but he, a phrase used to show his pride, like saying, " How grand
    he looked ! "

There is no one to equal George Herbert for homely and merry
wit, mingled with simplicity and holiness. The characters of the
tempters in this poem are shown in very few words : Glory that, " in
silks that whistled ", " scarce allowed me half an eye " ; and Wit that,
" to be short ", made an oration. " The Quip " means the clever
sarcastic jesting of the tempters.

74. Virtue

Sweet day, so cool, so calm, so bright,
The bridal of the earth and sky ;
The dew shall weep thy fall to-night,
    For thou must die.

Sweet rose, whose hue angry and brave
Bids the rash gazer wipe his eye ;
Thy root is ever in its grave,
    And thou must die.

Sweet spring, full of sweet days and roses,
A box where sweets compacted lie ;
My music shows ye have your closes,
    And all must die.

Only a sweet and virtuous soul,
Like seasoned timber, never gives ;
But though the whole world turn to coal,
    Then chiefly lives.

The Temple, 1633.   GEORGE HERBERT.

Compacted, fitted together.
Closes, end of a movement in music.

" And now scholar," says the fisherman in *The Compleat Angler*,
" my direction for fly-fishing is ended with this shower, for it has
done raining. And now look about you, and see how pleasantly that
meadow looks, nay and the earth smells as sweetly too. Come, let
me tell you what holy Mr. Herbert says of such days and flowers as
these, and then we will thank God that we enjoy them, and walk to
the river and sit down quietly, and try to catch the other brace of
trouts."

The poem is worth very careful studying, and particularly the way
in which the third verse summarizes the first two, and leads to the
point of the last verse, to the emphasis on lastingness and strength ;

the virtuous soul "like seasoned timber, never *gives*". So in the next poem Herbert insists on the value of energy, of restlessness. The holiness that he preaches in his poems is never mild or weak.

75. The Pulley

When God at first made man,
Having a glass of blessings standing by ;
"Let us," said he, " pour on him all we can :
Let the world's riches, which dispersèd lie,
    Contract into a span."

So strength first made a way ;
Then beauty flowed, then wisdom, honour, pleasure :
When almost all was out, God made a stay,
Perceiving that alone of all his treasure
    Rest in the bottom lay.

"For if I should," said he,
" Bestow this jewel also on my creature,
He would adore my works instead of me,
And rest in Nature, not the God of Nature :
    So both should losers be.

Yet let him keep the rest,
But keep them with repining restlessness ;
Let him be rich and weary, that at least
If goodness lead him not, yet weariness
    May toss him to my breast."

The Temple, 1633.   GEORGE HERBERT.

Why the title ?

[99]

76. Love

Love bade me welcome ; yet my soul drew back,
      Guilty of dust and sin.
But quick-eyed Love, observing me grow slack
      From my first entrance in,
Drew nearer to me, sweetly questioning,
      If I lacked anything.

" A guest," I answered, " worthy to be here."
      Love said, " You shall be he."
" I the unkind, ungrateful ? Ah my dear,
      I cannot look on thee."
Love took my hand, and smiling did reply,
      " Who made the eyes but I ? "

" Truth, Lord, but I have marred them : let my shame
      Go where it doth deserve."
" And know you not," says Love, " who bore the blame ? "
      " My dear, then I will serve."
" You must sit down," says Love, " and taste my meat."
      So I did sit and eat.

The Temple, 1633.   GEORGE HERBERT.

77

Oh sorrow, sorrow, say where thou dost dwell ?
  " In the lowest room of hell."
Art thou born of human race ?
  " No, no, I have a furier face."
Art thou in city, town, or court ?
  " I to every place resort."
Oh why into the world is sorrow sent ?
  " Men afflicted best repent."

What dost thou feed on?
  " Broken sleep."
What takest thou pleasure in?
  " To weep,
  To sigh, to sob, to pine, to groan,
  To wring my hands, to sit alone."
Oh when, oh when shall sorrow quiet have?
  " Never, never, never, never,
  Never till she finds a grave."

The Noble Spanish Soldier, 1634.   SAMUEL ROWLEY.

Furier, more like a fury. Some versions have " fairer " ; would this
   make better sense ?

Compare this way of describing Sorrow, by means of conversation,
with the Description of Virtue (No. 3). Try to make up one like
them on Joy (see poem No. 79), or Anger, or Greed.

78

O thou that sleep'st like pig in straw,
   Thou lady dear, arise !
Open (to keep the sun in awe)
   Thy pretty pinking eyes :
And, having stretched each leg and arm,
   Put on your clean white smock,
And then, I pray, to keep you warm,
   A petticoat on dock.

Arise, arise ! Why should you sleep
   When you have slept enough ?
Long since, French boys cried " Chimney-sweep ",
   And damsels " Kitchen-stuff ".
The shops were opened long before,
   And youngest prentice goes

To lay at 's mistress' chamber-door
  His master's shining shoes.

Arise, arise ! Your breakfast stays,
  Good water-gruel warm,
Or sugar-sops, which Galen says
  With mace will do no harm.
Arise, arise ! When you are up
  You'll find more to your cost,
For morning's-draught in caudle-cup,
  Good nut-brown ale and toast.

News from Plymouth, 1635.   SIR WILLIAM DAVENANT.

Pinking, piercing, beautiful.
Dock, back.
Galen, a Greek doctor of A.D. 200, whose medical books had been
    translated and were still in use in the seventeenth century.
Mace, nutmeg.
Caudle-cup, a warm drink.

The breakfast that awaits the lady is not very substantial. Most
people had even less : " Our breakfast in the morning," says a school-
boy, " is a little piece of bread, and a little butter, or some fruit, accord-
ing to the season of the year," and always a drink of ale with it.
  The confident sea-captain Topsail, who sings this song, is standing
below the lady's window with his musicians, who play the accom-
paniment.

79

My limbs I will fling
  Out of joint, and sing,
And dancing will shake my hair ;
  Not bow at each beck,
  Nor break my neck
With sorrow and deep despair.

Such a chirping din,
With mirth within,
And a head not needing a clout,
Is much better far
Than a careful chair
And a wreath of thorns without.

The Floating Island.   WILLIAM STRODE.

Clout, covering.

80

Why so pale and wan, fond lover?
  Prithee why so pale?
Will, when looking well can't move her,
  Looking ill prevail?
  Prithee why so pale?

Why so dull and mute, young sinner?
  Prithee why so mute?
Will, when speaking well can't win her,
  Saying nothing do 't?
  Prithee why so mute?

Quit, quit, for shame, this will not move,
  This cannot take her;
If of herself she will not love,
  Nothing can make her;
  The devil take her!

Aglaura, 1638.   SIR JOHN SUCKLING.

Compare this poem with Nos. 1, 5. Do you prefer Wyatt's
attitude, or Suckling's?

We show no monstrous crocodile,
Nor any prodigy of Nile ;
No Remora that stops your fleet,
Like serjeant's gallants in the street ;
No sea-horse which can trot or pace,
Or swim false gallop, post, or race.
For crooked dolphins we not care,
Though on their back a fiddler were.
The like to this fish which we show,
Was ne'er in Fish-street, old or new ;
Nor ever served to the sheriff's board,
Or kept in souse for the Mayor Lord.
Had old astronomers but seen
This fish, none else in heaven had been . . .

The City Match, 1639.   JASPER MAYNE.

   " Within this place is to be seen
   A wondrous fish. God save the Queen."
   " Why the Queen ? "
   " That was to make the rhyme."

Some practical jokers have taken rich Seathrift's son, given him a drink that makes him sleepy, and show him at the fair as " a rare sea-monster ". He wakens up just at the wrong moment, before the song is really finished, but with desperate patter they just save the situation.

The song gives a list of other remarkable fish, such as the Remora that clings to ships (like the " sergeant's gallants " that arrested criminals), and the dolphin on which Arion, the sweet singer, escaped from some sailors that wished to kill him. Poem No. **57** gives a list of similar wonders that attracted the people ; and in Shakespeare's *Tempest*, when Trinculo sees the savage Caliban, he thinks he is a fish, and says : " Were I in England now, and had but this fish painted, not a holiday fool there but would give me a piece of silver . . . When they will not give a doit to relieve a lame beggar, they will lay out ten to see a dead Indian."

The glories of our blood and state
  Are shadows, not substantial things ;
There is no armour against fate ;
  Death lays his icy hand on kings.
      Sceptre and crown
      Must tumble down,
And in the dust be equal made
With the poor crooked scythe and spade.

Some men with swords may reap the field,
  And plant fresh laurels where they kill ;
But their strong nerves at last must yield ;
  They tame but one another still ;
      Early or late,
      They stoop to fate,
And must give up their murmuring breath,
When they, pale captives, creep to death.

The garlands wither on your brow,
  Then boast no more your mighty deeds ;
Upon Death's purple altar now,
  See where the victor-victim bleeds :
      Your heads must come
      To the cold tomb ;
Only the actions of the just
Smell sweet, and blossom in their dust.

The Contention of Ajax and Ulysses
  for the Armour of Achilles.   JAMES SHIRLEY.

This was one of the most popular songs of the century, and a favourite one of Charles II. There is scarcely a line without some strong and effective phrase in it, such as " icy hand ", " creep to death ", " victor-victim ". Shirley was one of the last play-writers before the Puritans closed the theatres, but his songs show no lack of power or of poetry.

83. Epigram : On Sir Francis Drake

Sir Drake, whom well the world's end knew,
　　Which thou didst compass round,
And whom both poles of heaven once saw
　　Which north and south do bound,
The stars above would make thee known,
　　If men here silent were ;
The sun himself cannot forget
　　His fellow traveller.

Wit's Recreations, 1640.　　　　　　　ANONYMOUS.

It is a great tribute to Sir Francis Drake, and to the fame of his great
voyage round the world, that poems were still written in praise of
him more than forty years after his death.

84

If all the world were paper,
　　And all the sea were ink,
And all the trees were bread and cheese,
　　How should we do for drink ?

If all the world were sand-o,
　　Oh, then what should we lack-o ?
If, as they say, there were no clay,
　　How should we take tobacco ?

If all our vessels ran-a,
　　If none but had a crack-a ;
If Spanish apes ate all the grapes,
　　How should we do for sack-a ?

[106]

If friars had no bald pates,
  Nor nuns had no dark cloisters ;
If all the seas were beans and peas,
  How should we do for oysters ?

If there had been no projects,
  Nor none that did great wrongs ;
If fiddlers shall turn players all,
  How should we do for songs ?

If all things were eternal,
  And nothing their end bringing ;
If this should be, then how should we
  Here make an end of singing ?

Wit's Recreations, 1641.   ANONYMOUS.

This nonsense poem was perhaps inspired by an earlier love-song—

  " If all the earth were paper white
    And all the sea were ink,
  'Twere not enough for me to write
    As my poor heart doth think."

But we can probably be glad that it was the nonsense poem that was
finished and survives, and not the love-poem.

85. Song of the Beggars

From hunger and cold who lives more free,
  Or who more richly clad than we ?
Our bellies are full ; our flesh is warm ;
  And, against pride, our rags are a charm.
Enough is our feast, and for to-morrow
  Let rich men care ; we feel no sorrow.
    No sorrow, no sorrow, no sorrow, no sorrow,
    Let rich men care, we feel no sorrow.

Each city, each town, and every village
  Affords us either an alms or pillage.
And if the weather be cold or raw,
  Then, in a barn we tumble in straw ;
If warm and fair, by yea-cock and nay-cock
  The fields will afford us a hedge or a hay-cock :
    A hay-cock, a hay-cock, a hay-cock, a hay-cock,
    The fields will afford us a hedge or a hay-cock.

A Jovial Crew. RICHARD BROME.

Beggars' songs were very popular ; but no one could tell from
this cheerful one that it comes in the last play to be acted in the theatres,
before Parliament closed them in 1642. " It had the luck ", as an old
writer puts it, " to tumble last of all in the epidemical ruin of the scene."

86. Go, lovely rose

  Go, lovely rose,
Tell her that wastes her time and me,
  That now she knows,
When I resemble her to thee,
How sweet and fair she seems to be.

  Tell her that's young,
And shuns to have her graces spied,
  That hadst thou sprung
In deserts where no men abide,
Thou must have uncommended died.

  Small is the worth
Of beauty from the light retired ;
  Bid her come forth,

Suffer herself to be desired,
And not blush so to be admired.

Then die, that she
The common fate of all things rare
May read in thee,
How small a part of time they share
That are so wondrous sweet and fair.

Poems, 1645.   EDMUND WALLER.

87

. . . Yet if his majesty, our sovereign lord,
Should of his own accord
Friendly himself invite,
And say "I'll be your guest to-morrow night,"
How should we stir ourselves, call and command
All hands to work! "Let no man idle stand.

Set me fine Spanish tables in the hall,
See they be fitted all;
Let there be room to eat,
And order taken that there want no meat.
See every sconce and candlestick made bright,
That without tapers they may give a light.

Look to the presence: are the carpets spread,
The dazie o'er the head,
The cushions in the chairs,
And all the candles lighted on the stairs?
Perfume the chambers, and in any case
Let each man give attendance in his place."

Thus if the king were coming would we do ;
And 'twere good reason too ;
For 'tis a duteous thing
To show all honour to an earthly king ;
And, after all our travail and our cost,
So he be pleased, to think no labour lost.

But at the coming of the King of Heaven
All's set at six and seven ;
We wallow in our sin ;
Christ cannot find a chamber in the inn.
We entertain him always like a stranger,
And, as at first, still lodge him in the manger.

ANONYMOUS.

Sconce, candlestick on the wall.
Dazie, a canopy, such as only kings had over their thrones.

This poem, from a manuscript in Oxford, begins curiously, and
may be part of a longer poem. But the sense is complete and the
construction is beautifully worked out. It is not until the last word
of all that the real point comes.

Which word gives the first hint of what the moral is going to be ?

88

" Say, bold but blessed thief,
That in a trice
Slipped into paradise,
And in plain day
Stol'st heaven away,
What trick couldst thou invent
To compass thy intent ?
What arms ?
What charms ? "
" Love and belief."

[110]

"Say, bold but blessed thief,
How couldst thou read
A crown upon that head?
What text, what gloss,
A kingdom on a cross?
How couldst thou come to spy
God in a man to die?
What light?
What sight?"
"The sight of grief—

I sight to God his pain;
And by that sight
I saw the light;
Thus did my grief
Beget relief.
And take this rule from me,
Pity thou him he'll pity thee.
Use this,
Ne'er miss,
Heaven may be stol'n again."

ANONYMOUS.

I sight, I sighed.

"And there were also two other, malefactors, led with him to be put to death. . . . And one of the malefactors which were hanged railed on him, saying: 'If thou be the Christ, save thyself and us!' But the other answering rebuked him, saying: 'Dost not thou fear God, seeing thou art in the same condemnation? And we indeed justly; for we receive the due reward of our deeds; but this man hath done nothing amiss.'

And he said unto Jesus: 'Lord, remember me when thou comest into thy kingdom!' And Jesus said unto him, 'Verily I say unto thee, To-day shalt thou be with me in paradise.' "—*Luke*, xxiii. 32, 39–43.

[111]

A Thanksgiving to God, for his House

Lord, thou hast given me a cell
  Wherein to dwell ;
A little house, whose humble roof
  Is weather-proof ;
Under the spars of which I lie
  Both soft, and dry ;
Where thou my chamber for to ward
  Hast set a guard
Of harmless thoughts, to watch and keep
  Me, while I sleep.
Low is my porch, as is my fate,
  Both void of state ;
And yet the threshold of my door
  Is worn by the poor,
Who thither come, and freely get
  Good words, or meat.
Like as my parlour, so my hall
  And kitchen's small :
A little buttery, and therein
  A little bin,
Which keeps my little loaf of bread
  Unchipt, unflead.
Some brittle sticks of thorn or briar
  Make me a fire,
Close by whose living coal I sit,
  And glow like it.
Lord, I confess too, when I dine,
  The pulse is thine,
And all those other bits, that be
  There placed by thee :
The worts, the purslain, and the mess
  Of watercress,

Which of thy kindness thou hast sent;
  And my content
Makes those, and my beloved beet,
  To be more sweet.
'Tis thou that crown'st my glittering hearth
  With guiltless mirth;
And giv'st me wassail-bowls to drink,
  Spic'd to the brink.
Lord, 'tis thy plenty-dropping hand,
  That soils my land,
And giv'st me, for my bushel sown,
  Twice ten for one:
Thou mak'st my teeming hen to lay
  Her egg each day,
Besides my healthful ewes to bear
  Me twins each year,
The while the conduits of my kine
  Run cream (for wine).
All these, and better thou dost send
  Me, to this end,
That I should render, for my part,
  A thankful heart;
Which, fir'd with incense, I resign,
  As wholly thine;
But the acceptance, that must be,
  My Christ, by thee.

His Noble Numbers, 1647.   ROBERT HERRICK.

Buttery, pantry.
Unflead, unbroken, with the crust still on.
Pulse, beans or peas.
Worts, purslain, herbs used in salads.

Herrick spent part of his life in London, part of it as the parson
in a little Devonshire village. Although he often complains of the

dullness of country life, such a poem as this seems to show that he was
really contented and happy there.

90. To Meadows

Ye have been fresh and green,
  Ye have been filled with flowers,
And ye the walks have been
  Where maids have spent their hours.

You have beheld, how they
  With wicker arks did come
To kiss, and bear away
  The richer cowslips home.

You have heard them sweetly sing,
  And seen them in a round :
Each virgin, like a spring,
  With honey-suckles crowned.

But now we see none here,
  Whose silvery feet did tread,
And with dishevelled hair
  Adorned this smoother mead.

Like unthrifts, having spent
  Your stock, and needy grown,
You are left here to lament
  Your poor estates, alone.

Hesperides, 1648.   ROBERT HERRICK.

Arks, baskets.

[114]

91. The Night-piece, to Julia

Her eyes the glow-worm lend thee,
The shooting stars attend thee ;
  And the elves also,
  Whose little eyes glow
Like the sparks of fire, befriend thee.

No will-o'-th'-wisp mislight thee ;
Nor snake or slow-worm bite thee,
  But on, on thy way
  Not making a stay,
Since ghost there's none to affright thee.

Let not the dark thee cumber ;
What though the moon does slumber ?
  The stars of the night
  Will lend thee their light,
Like tapers clear without number.

Then Julia let me woo thee,
Thus, thus to come unto me ;
  And when I shall meet
  Thy silvery feet,
My soul I'll pour into thee.

Hesperides, 1648.   ROBERT HERRICK.

Did Herrick get the idea and the metre of this poem from Ben
Jonson's first Gipsy Song (No. 58) ? Read one after the other, and
they might almost make up one poem. But Herrick's wishes for a
safe journey at night lead up to his last verse, when the lovers meet ;
and his words are more carefully chosen for their romantic and gentle
sound than Jonson's are.

92. His Poetry His Pillar

Only a little more
  I have to write,
   Then I'll give o'er,
And bid the world good-night.

'Tis but a flying minute,
  That I must stay
   Or linger in it ;
And then I must away.

O Time that cutt'st down all !
  And scarce leav'st here
   Memorial
Of any men that were.

How many lie forgot
  In vaults beneath,
   And piece-meal rot
Without a fame in death ?

Behold this living stone
  I rear for me,
   Ne'er to be thrown
Down, envious Time, by thee.

Pillars let some set up,
  (If so they please)
   Here is my hope,
And my Pyramidès.

Hesperides, 1648.   ROBERT HERRICK.

Yet envious Time all but threw down his pyramids ; for nearly
a century and a half his poems lay " without a fame in death ". Not
until 1796 was his name recalled to mind and his gift of song recognized.

93. To Daffodils

Fair daffodils, we weep to see
  You haste away so soon :
As yet the early-rising sun
  Has not attained his noon.
      Stay, stay,
  Until the hasting day
        Has run
  But to the even-song ;
And, having prayed together, we
  Will go with you along.

We have short time to stay, as you,
  We have as short a spring ;
As quick a growth to meet decay
  As you, or any thing.
      We die,
  As your hours do, and dry
        Away,
  Like to the summer's rain ;
Or as the pearls of morning's dew
  Ne'er to be found again.

Hesperides, 1648.   Robert Herrick.

After reading this poem through once or twice, try to work out the arrangement of the lines and the rhymes. The scheme is most complicated, and yet the two verses correspond almost exactly, and with no feeling of strained cleverness.

Here is Herrick on the same subject, but in a less lyrical mood.

> " When a daffodil I see,
> Hanging down his head towards me,
> Guess I may what I must be :
> First, I shall decline my head ;
> Secondly, I shall be dead ;
> Lastly, safely burièd."

[117]

94. To Lucasta, Going to the Wars

Tell me not, sweet, I am unkind,
   That from the nunnery
Of thy chaste breast and quiet mind
   To war and arms I fly.

True, a new mistress now I chase,
   The first foe in the field,
And with a stronger faith embrace
   A sword, a horse, a shield.

Yet this inconstancy is such,
   As you too shall adore ;
I could not love thee, dear, so much,
   Loved I not honour more.

Lucasta, 1649.   RICHARD LOVELACE.

Much of Lovelace's life was spent in fighting for the Royalists in the Civil War, or in the Roundheads' prison. He wrote much verse, but only a few of his songs have the real ring of poetry. For the rest of his verse he is

   " The foolishest poet that ever I redd
      Put out ye candle I'le to bedd."

95. Peace

My soul, there is a country
   Far beyond the stars,
Where stands a wingèd sentry
   All skilful in the wars ;
There, above noise and danger,
   Sweet peace sits crowned with smiles,

[118]

And one born in a manger
  Commands the beauteous files.
He is thy gracious friend,
  And (O my soul awake !)
Did in pure love descend
  To die here for thy sake ;
If thou canst get but thither,
  There grows the flower of peace,
The rose that cannot wither,
  Thy fortress, and thy ease.
Leave then thy foolish ranges ;
  For none can thee secure,
But one, who never changes,
  Thy God, thy life, thy cure.

Silex Scintillans, 1650.   HENRY VAUGHAN.

Files, army.
Ranges, wanderings.

  Even if he had not told us himself, we should have known that
Henry Vaughan revered "the blessed man, Mr. George Herbert,
whose holy life and verse gained many pious converts, of whom I am
the least ". He has the same simplicity and the same range of subjects.

96. The Retreat

Happy those early days ! when I
Shined in my angel-infancy.
Before I understood this place
Appointed for my second race,
Or taught my soul to fancy aught
But a white, celestial thought ;
When yet I had not walked above
A mile or two from my first love,

[119]

And (looking back) at that short space
Could see a glimpse of his bright face ;
When on some gilded cloud or flower
My gazing soul would dwell an hour,
And in those weaker glories spy
Some shadows of eternity ;
Before I taught my tongue to wound
My conscience with a sinful sound,
Or had the black art to dispense
A several sin to every sense,
But felt through all this fleshly dress
Bright shoots of everlastingness.

   Oh, how I long to travel back
And tread again that ancient track !
That I might once more reach that plain,
Where first I left my glorious train,
From whence the enlightened spirit sees
That shady city of palm trees ;
But ah ! my soul with too much stay
Is drunk, and staggers in the way.
Some men a forward motion love,
But I by backward steps would move,
And when this dust falls to the urn,
In that state I came, return.

Silex Scintillans, 1650.   HENRY VAUGHAN.

My first love, Christ.
Several, separate.

    " There was a time when meadow, grove and stream,
      The earth and every common sight
          To me did seem
        Apparelled in celestial light,
      The glory and the freshness of a dream."

So William Wordsworth, a century and a half later than Vaughan,
begins a great poem on the same subject of the innocence of child-

[120]

hood. The memories that men have of this, the "shadows of eternity"
and "bright shoots of everlastingness" that they feel, are described
by Wordsworth as being like a distant view on a clear day—

> " Hence in a season of calm weather
>   Though inland far we be,
>   Our souls have sight of that immortal sea
>   Which brought us hither,
>   Can in a moment travel thither,
> And see the children sport upon the shore,
> And hear the mighty waters rolling evermore."

97. De Morte

Man's life's a tragedy. His mother's womb
(From which he enters) is the tiring-room ;
This spacious earth the theatre ; and the stage
That country which he lives in ; passions, rage,
Folly, and vice are actors ; the first cry
The prologue to the ensuing tragedy.
The former act consisteth of dumb shows ;
The second, he to more perfection grows ;
I' th' third he is a man, and doth begin
To nurture vice, and act the deeds of sin ;
I' th' fourth declines ; i' th' fifth diseases clog
And trouble him ; then Death's his epilogue.

Reliquiæ Wottonianae.   ANONYMOUS.

Epilogue, the conclusion of the play.

The author of this poem (we do not know his name) must have
read Raleigh's poem (No. 50), and found that there were many more
points in which man's life is like a play.   Compare the two carefully
and decide which one you prefer.   In a modern theatre, to what might
you compare the make-up, the scenery, the critics, the manager of
the theatre ?

98. The Coronet

When for the thorns with which I long, too long,
    With many a piercing wound,
    My Saviour's head have crowned,
I seek with garlands to redress that wrong,
    Through every garden, every mead,
I gather flowers (my fruits are only flowers)
    Dismantling all the fragrant towers
That once adorned my shepherdess's head.
And now when I have summed up all my store,
    Thinking (so I myself deceive)
    So rich a chaplet thence to weave
As never yet the king of glory wore,
    Alas ! I find the Serpent old
    That, twining in his speckled breast,
    About the flowers disguised does fold
    With wreaths of fame and interest.
Ah, foolish man, that wouldst debase with them,
And mortal glory, Heaven's diadem !
But thou who only couldst the Serpent tame,
Either his slippery knots at once untie,
And disentangle all his winding snare ;
Or shatter too with him my curious frame,
And let these wither—so that he may die—
Though set with skill, and chosen out with care ;
That they, while Thou on both their spoils dost tread,
May crown thy feet, that could not crown thy head.

Miscellaneous Poems.   ANDREW MARVELL.

Marvell and Milton were the only Puritans that were really out-
standing as poets. Marvell was a most business-like Member of
Parliament for Hull, and a true patriot ; but his best poems were
written earlier, about 1650, when he was a private tutor at Nun
Appleton House in Yorkshire.

99. A Contemplation upon Flowers

Brave flowers, that I could gallant it like you
And be as little vain ;
You come abroad, and make a harmless show,
And to your beds of earth again ;
You are not proud, you know your birth
For your embroidered garments are from earth.

You do obey your months and times, but I
Would have it ever spring ;
My fate would know no winter, never die
Nor think of such a thing ;
O that I could my bed of earth but view,
And smile, and look as cheerfully as you.

O teach me to see death, and not to fear
But rather to take truce.
How often have I seen you at a bier,
And there look fresh and spruce ;
You fragrant flowers, then teach me that my breath
Like yours may sweeten, and perfume my death.

BISHOP KING.

100

The lark now leaves his watery nest
    And climbing shakes his dewy wings.
He takes this window for the east,
    And to implore your light he sings,
Awake, awake, the morn will never rise
Till she can dress her beauty at your eyes.

The merchant bows unto the seaman's star,
  The ploughman from the sun his season takes ;
But still the lover wonders what they are
  Who look for day before his mistress wakes.
Awake, awake, break through your veils of lawn !
Then draw your curtains, and begin the dawn.

                              SIR WILLIAM DAVENANT.

Bows unto, obeys.

Davenant was treated like a son by Shakespeare ; he succeeded Ben
Jonson as Poet Laureate in 1638 ; was saved by Milton from imprison-
ment during the Commonwealth ; and after the restoration of Charles II,
in 1660, he became a friend of Dryden and one of the chief play-
writers in London.   So, although he is no great poet, he was a friend
of the greatest poets of the century, and links up the first half with the
second.

   This poem, in its freshness and simple wording, might almost have
been written in Elizabeth's reign.   Compare it with *Sister awake*
(No. 35), and *O thou that sleep'st* (No. 78), and see what differences
you can find.

Index of First Lines

Page

All this night shrill chanticler 92
All ye woods, and trees and bowers 64
Arm, arm, arm, arm ! the scouts are all come in . . 76
A rose, as fair as ever saw the north 93
Art thou poor, yet hast thou golden slumbers . . . 55
As inward love breeds outward talk 52
Autumn hath all the summer's fruitful treasure . . . 40

Beauty sat bathing by a spring 46
Behold, a silly tender babe 38
Brave flowers, that I could gallant it like you . . . 123

Call for the robin-redbreast and the wren 70
Come away, come away, death 44
Come live with me and be my love 35
Cupid and my Campaspe played 23

Each month hath praise in some degree 42

Fain would I change that note 60
Fair daffodils, we weep to see 117
Farewell rewards and fairies 89
Fear no more the heat o' the sun 65
Fly hence, shadows, that do keep 93
Fools, they are the only nation 61
From hunger and cold who lives more free . . . 107
Full fathom five thy father lies 69

Give me my scallop-shell of quiet 57
Give place, ye lovers here before 21
Golden slumbers kiss your eyes 54
Go, lovely rose 108
Gorbo, as thou camest this way 47
Greensleeves was all my joy 24

	Page
Happy those early days ! when I	119
Happy were he could finish forth his fate . . .	42
Hark, now everything is still	85
Haymakers, rakers, reapers, and mowers . . .	87
Hence all you vain delights.	88
Her eyes the glow-worm lend thee	115
I am two fools, I know	39
If all the world and love were young	36
If all the world were paper	106
In the merry month of May	33
Jack and Joan they think no ill	73
Lay a garland on my hearse	68
Let not the sluggish sleep	68
Like to the damask rose you see	95
Lord, thou hast given me a cell	112
Love bade me welcome ; yet my soul drew back . .	100
Maids to bed, and cover coal	68
Man's life's a tragedy. His mother's womb. . . .	121
My golden locks time hath to silver turned . . .	32
My limbs I will fling	102
My lute, awake ! perform the last	19
My prime of life is but a frost of cares . . .	29
My soul, there is a country	118
Now winter nights enlarge	74
Oh sorrow, sorrow, say where thou dost dwell ? . .	100
Only a little more	116
O thou that sleep'st like pig in straw	101
Queen and huntress, chaste, and fair	45
Ring out your bells, let mourning shows be spread . .	27
Roses, their sharp spines being gone	72
Say, bold but blessed thief	110
Shepherds all, and maidens fair	63
Sigh no more, ladies, sigh no more	41

Page
Sir Drake, whom well the world's end knew 106
Sister awake, close not your eyes 59
Slow, slow, fresh fount ; keep time with my salt tears 44
So, now is come our joyful'st feast 80
Spring, the sweet spring, is the year's pleasant king . 34
Sweet day, so cool, so calm, so bright 98
Sweet Suffolk owl, so trimly dight 78
Sweet was the song the Virgin sung 84
Tell me not, sweet, I am unkind 118
The faery beam upon you 79
The glories of our blood and state 105
The Indian weed withered quite 66
The lark now leaves his watery nest 123
The man of life upright 51
The merry world did on a day 96
There is a garden in her face 62
The sea hath many thousand sands 67
This world a hunting is 85
Thule, the period of cosmography 49
To his sweet lute Apollo sung the motions of the spheres . 75
To see a strange outlandish fowl 78
Underneath this marble hearse 84
Weep with me all you that read 70
Weep you no more sad fountains 56
We show no monstrous crocodile 104
What is our life ? A play of passion 71
What one art thou, thus in torn weeds yclad ? . . . 22
What pleasure have great princes 30
Whenas the chill Charocco blows 94
When for the thorns with which I long, too long . . 122
When God at first made man 99
When icicles hang by the wall 37
When thou must home to shades of underground . . 50
When to her lute Corinna sings 50
Why so pale and wan, fond lover ? 103
Wilt thou forgive that sin, where I begun . . . 98
Ye have been fresh and green 114
Yet if his majesty, our sovereign lord 109